SCIENCE ADVENTURES

Solve the puzzles, save the world!

ARCTURUS

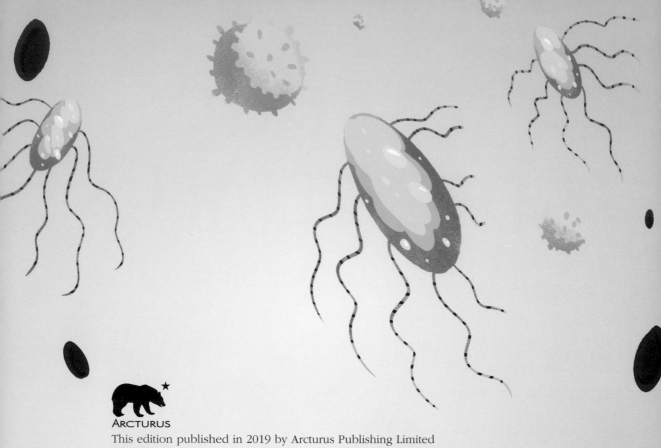

Arcturus

This edition published in 2019 by Arcturus Publishing Limited
26/27 Bickels Yard, 151–153 Bermondsey Street,
London SE1 3HA

Author: Alex Woolf
Illustrator: Geraldine Rodriguez
Editor: Rachel Cooke and Joe Harris
Designer: Stefan Holliland

ISBN: 978-1-78888-736-6
CH006569NT
Supplier 29, Date 0819, Print run 8447

Printed in China

What is STEM?

STEM is a world-wide initiative
that aims to cultivate an
interest in Science, Technology,
Engineering, and Mathematics,
in an effort to promote these
disciplines to as wide a variety of
students as possible.

CONTENTS

HOW TO USE THIS BOOK

The interactive adventure stories in this book feature questions and puzzles on most pages.

When you reach a challenge, stop! To unlock the next part of the story, you must find the right answer. DON'T SKIP AHEAD until you've worked it out! Check that your solution is correct by turning to the answers section at the back of the book.

Watch for the DATA BLAST pages in each chapter. These are packed with science facts and explanations. Read them carefully, because they will help you later on. If you don't know the answer to a question, turn back to the previous Data Blast page.

CHAPTER 1

THE INCREDIBLE BODY ODYSSEY

One day, schoolgirl Anna Tomical receives an unexpected call. "Who is it?" asks her friend Hugh. "It's my great-uncle, the world-famous scientist, Professor Barrington Bone!" The Professor summons them to his lab to see his latest invention.

How can we help?

Anna and Hugh rush to the lab. There, they are met not by Professor Bone, but by his assistant, Justin Jectem. Justin looks very worried. "The professor's great rival, Belinda Blood, has injected a tiny robot into his bloodstream! It's made him very sick!"

This is the Microship.

"The only way to save Professor Bone is to use his latest invention, a Microship," says Justin. "It's a shrinking submarine that can travel inside people's bodies. You will need to pilot the Microship through his body, while I give you instructions."

Anna and Hugh climb on board the Microship, and Justin presses a button on a control panel in the lab. *ZAAAAAP!* Suddenly, the kids find themselves in a red tunnel.

"This must be a vein," says Anna. All around them are red blood cells, floating in a clear liquid. They hear Justin's voice crackling over an intercom system.

"To catch the "SickBot," you'll need to head for the heart."

Is it this way?

Which way does blood travel in veins? Does it go to or from the heart?

If you don't know ... then turn the page for your first DATA BLAST!

Before you set off, let's refresh what you know about circulation. The Microship's computer will bring you up to speed!

DATA BLAST

CIRCULATION is the body's internal transport system. It includes the blood, blood vessels, and heart. Blood is made up of red and white blood cells and platelets. They all float in a watery liquid called plasma.

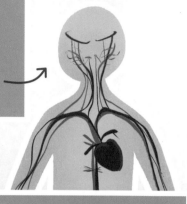

RED BLOOD CELLS carry oxygen to the body's cells, and carry carbon dioxide from the cells back to the lungs.

WHITE BLOOD CELLS fight disease. They work together to attack bacteria and viruses.

PLATELETS help blood to clot (become sticky) when you get a cut. They form a mesh over the wound that will eventually form a scab.

The **HEART** is the organ that pumps blood. It has four chambers—right atrium, right ventricle, left atrium, and left ventricle. Oxygen-poor blood from the body arrives in the right atrium, then moves to the right ventricle. From here it is sent along the pulmonary artery to the lungs to receive oxygen. The oxygen-rich blood then travels back to the heart's left atrium, passes to the left ventricle and then is pumped out to the rest of the body.

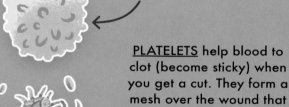

The blood cells and platelets float in a liquid called **PLASMA**. Plasma contains chemicals called antibodies, which help shield the body from disease.

BLOOD VESSELS are tubes that carry blood. There are three types. Arteries carry blood away from the heart in fast surges. Veins carry blood back to the heart. Tiny blood vessels called capillaries link up the veins and arteries and carry blood to and from the body's cells.

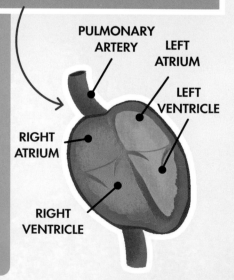

PULMONARY ARTERY

LEFT ATRIUM

LEFT VENTRICLE

RIGHT ATRIUM

RIGHT VENTRICLE

The Microship makes a sputtering noise. Hugh notices a flashing light on the control panel. "We'll need oxygen for fuel! But don't red blood cells carry oxygen?"

"Not always ... " says Anna. "They sometimes carry carbon dioxide."

Which gas do red blood cells carry in arteries to the body's cells? Which gas do they carry in veins from the cells back to the lungs?

Just then, a white blood cell appears. These cells attack invaders ... including Microships!

"Look, there's a camouflage setting!" says Anna. "But what should we disguise ourselves as?"

Should they disguise the ship as a bacterium or an antibody?

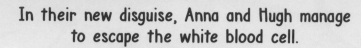

In their new disguise, Anna and Hugh manage to escape the white blood cell.

Unfortunately, in all the excitement, they take a wrong turn. They race down narrow, branching passages, until the Microship gets stuck!

Push harder!

Eventually, Anna and Hugh free the Microship. "That's a relief," says Hugh. "But where are we? What is this vessel?"

Are they in a vein or artery? Or somewhere else?

Anna and Hugh eventually manage to reach a larger blood vessel. The blood here is moving much faster than before, in powerful surges. But the Microship's blinking control panel says they are very low on fuel.

Justin's voice crackles over the intercom again. "Those blood cells are carrying oxygen," he says. "You could use them to refuel."

"But are we going the right way to get to the heart?" asks Anna.

What kind of blood vessel are they now in? Will it take them to the heart?

Bad news! They're in an artery, which means they are moving away from the heart.

They must return through the capillaries and find a vein. But something is wrong. The blood is rushing faster than usual. They see light ahead of them. Blood is pouring out of a hole in the skin!

What makes blood become sticky?

What things within blood help it clot?

Has Professor Bone grazed himself, or is this the work of the SickBot?

"It's okay," says Anna, "the blood will soon become sticky and form a mesh over the wound."

"That doesn't seem to be happening," says Hugh. "Something is wrong."

The SickBot has done something to Professor Bone's blood and it isn't clotting. Anna and Hugh must act quickly. They climb out of the Microship and begin pushing special parts of the blood to the wound site. Soon, a mesh has formed over the wound.

Leaving the graze behind, Anna and Hugh race along a vein to the heart.

"We need to catch the SickBot before it causes any more trouble!" says Anna.

If the SickBot has been interfering with the heart ...

... it could still be nearby!

How many chambers do we need to search?

How many chambers does the heart have? What are their names?

Anna and Hugh enter the heart's right atrium through a valve. From here they move swiftly through another valve into the right ventricle. However, they can't see the SickBot anywhere.

Suddenly, everything starts shaking. They can hear a deep coughing and choking. Professor Bone is struggling to breathe. The SickBot must have gone to his lungs!

"We're in the right ventricle of the heart," says Hugh. "But which chamber leads to the lungs?"

Which chamber of the heart leads to the lungs?

COUGH COUGH COUGH!

Another valve opens, pulling the Microship into a blood vessel.

"Wait!" shouts Anna. "The computer says this is the pulmonary artery. But does that lead to the lungs?"

"We have to decide quickly," cries Hugh. "We're getting dragged in there!"

Is this the right way?

My heart isn't set on it.

Where does the pulmonary artery lead?

15

Breathing is essential to life. If we stopped breathing, we would die in just a few minutes. We breath in oxygen from the air. Our cells need oxygen to take energy from our food into our body. This process produces a waste gas called carbon dioxide. We breathe out to get rid of carbon dioxide. Another word for breathing is respiration. The parts of the body we use for breathing are called the respiratory system. They include the mouth, nose, throat, larynx, trachea, and lungs.

NASAL PASSAGE

MOUTH

THROAT

TRACHEA

This is also known as the windpipe. It is a hollow tube that connects the throat to the lungs. The trachea is lined with thousands of tiny hairs called cilia. These trap dust and other particles from the air, preventing them from reaching the lungs. When we cough, we force these particles out of the trachea.

LARYNX

This is also known as the voicebox. It contains our vocal cords. When these are open, they make no sound. If we wish to speak, neck muscles pull the vocal cords closer together. As air flows through them, the vocal cords vibrate, producing sounds.

BRONCHI

BRONCHIOLE

ALVEOLI

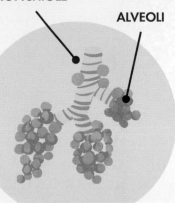

LUNGS

The trachea splits into two tubes called bronchi, one going to each lung. Inside the lungs, the bronchi divide into a network of smaller tubes called bronchioles. At the end of the smallest bronchioles are tiny, bumpy air sacs called alveoli (one is an alveolus). Wound around the alveoli are capillaries. These bring blood to the lungs to be recharged with oxygen from the alveoli (and then sent back to the heart for pumping around the body). The capillaries also release carbon dioxide into the alveoli to be breathed out. Alveoli and capillaries have walls thin enough for tiny gas molecules to pass through.

The Microship shoots along the pulmonary artery and enters a network of tiny capillaries. Finally, the kids find themselves looking at a hollow object with a bumpy surface, which keeps growing bigger, then smaller.

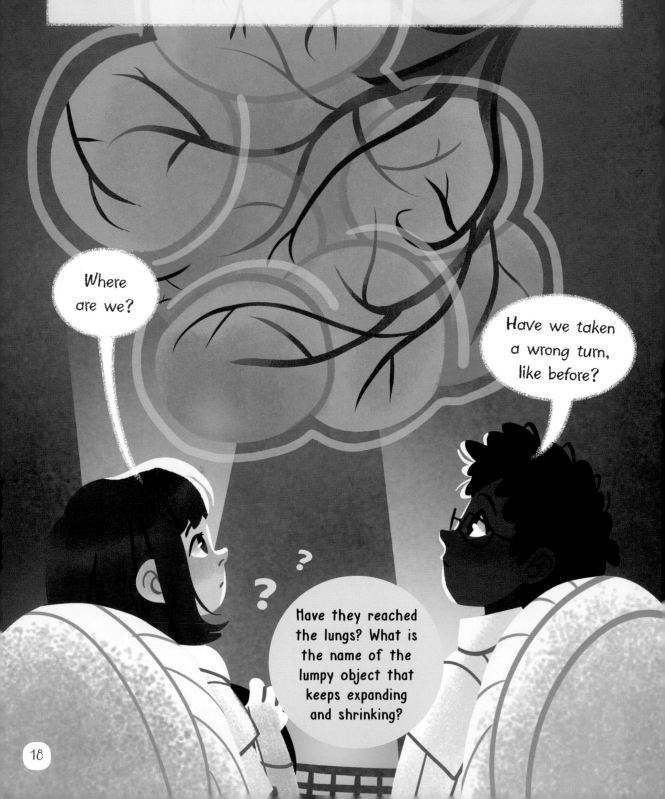

Where are we?

Have we taken a wrong turn, like before?

Have they reached the lungs? What is the name of the lumpy object that keeps expanding and shrinking?

Anna and Hugh pilot the Microship through a capillary, right up to the hollow object … but they can't get inside. There's a wall blocking their route!

"I'm sure something is getting through the wall," says Anna. "It's causing the dark blood cells in this capillary to become bright red."

"We saw bright red blood cells before," says Hugh, "when we were in the artery. They look like that when they're carrying a gas."

What gas are bright red blood cells filled with?

"So gases can move through the wall. To follow, we'll have to get even smaller!" says Anna.

What gas is moving from the chamber into the capillary? What gas is moving through the wall in the opposite direction?

Anna presses the "shrink" button on the control panel. The Microship becomes even tinier, and passes through the wall of the alveolus. Once through, it expands again.

They are now inside the lungs' airways, and it's a very windy place! They keep getting blown about, but they manage to force their way out of the alveolus and into a series of narrow tubes.

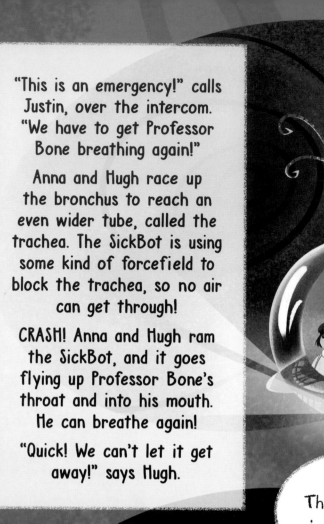

"This is an emergency!" calls Justin, over the intercom. "We have to get Professor Bone breathing again!"

Anna and Hugh race up the bronchus to reach an even wider tube, called the trachea. The SickBot is using some kind of forcefield to block the trachea, so no air can get through!

CRASH! Anna and Hugh ram the SickBot, and it goes flying up Professor Bone's throat and into his mouth. He can breathe again!

"Quick! We can't let it get away!" says Hugh.

This is a pain in the neck!

But they can't follow the SickBot. They keep getting stuck on the hairy, sticky walls of the trachea.

What are these hairs and how can they escape them?

Anna presses a button in the Microship marked "Tickler." Professor Bone coughs, freeing them from the hairs.

COUGH COUGH!

The Microship flies upward and crashes against a pair of fleshy doors. Air from the lungs is flowing through the gap between the doors, causing them to vibrate and make a deep, complicated sound.

How can we make them open?

What are these doors? What is the sound they're making? Can you think of a way to open them?

"Uncle Barrington must be talking," says Anna. "Justin, you have to stop him! That will open the vocal cords."

Justin tells Professor Bone to rest his voice.

Shhh!

A moment later, the vocal cords open and the Microship passes through the throat and into the mouth. There's no sign of the SickBot!

Then they hear a deep gurgle from far below! The SickBot must have gone to the stomach. Before they follow, the ship's computer uploads some more important info ...

MOUTH

THROAT

ESOPHAGUS

STOMACH

SMALL INTESTINE

LARGE INTESTINE

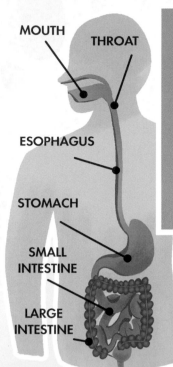

The body cannot use food as it is, so must break it down into simpler substances. This is called digestion. Most of the digestive system is a tube that travels through the body and includes the foodpipe, stomach, small intestine, and large intestine. Other organs that help digestion include the liver and pancreas.

DATA BLAST

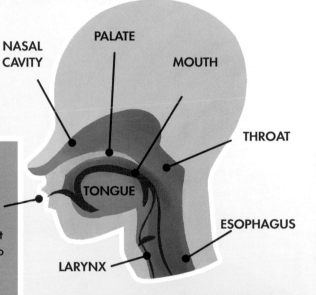

NASAL CAVITY

PALATE

MOUTH

THROAT

TONGUE

ESOPHAGUS

LARYNX

MOUTH AND FOODPIPE

The tongue tastes the food, teeth mash it, and saliva softens it. When the food is ready for swallowing, the tongue pushes it to the back of the mouth. The food touches the top of the throat and this causes flaps to close off the windpipe, so the food moves into the esophagus, a muscular tube that sends it to the stomach.

SMALL INTESTINE

This is a long, narrow tube coiled up inside the abdomen. Here, juices produced by the liver and pancreas help to further break down food into useful nutrients. These are absorbed into the body through the lining of the small intestine. Juice from the pancreas also contains a chemical to protect the small intestine from stomach acid.

STOMACH

This is a bag-like organ with wrinkled, muscular walls that stretch to make space for a meal. Glands in the stomach wall make an acidic liquid called gastric juice (stomach acid) that helps break down the food.

APPENDIX

LARGE INTESTINE

What's left of the food is waste matter, which passes into the large intestine. Here, water is absorbed from the waste, and the remaining solids leave the body when you go to the toilet. Attached to the first part of the large intestine is a long, thin pouch called the appendix. This has no important function.

25

"We need to get to the stomach," says Anna.

"The Professor will have to swallow us," says Hugh. "Let's move to the back of the mouth."

Anna presses the accelerator, but the Microship doesn't move. "We seem to be stuck!" she says.

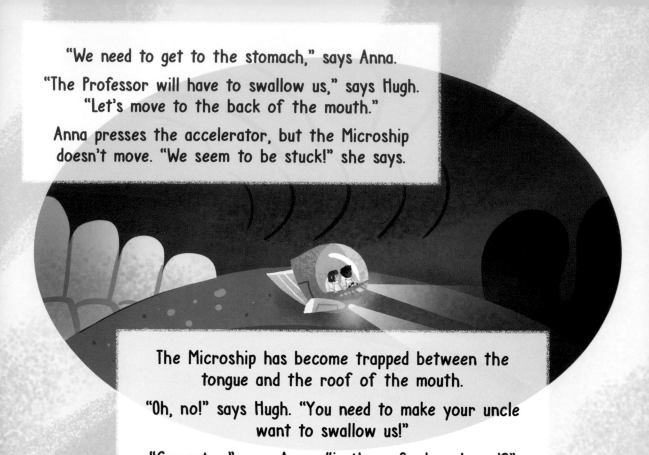

The Microship has become trapped between the tongue and the roof of the mouth.

"Oh, no!" says Hugh. "You need to make your uncle want to swallow us!"

"Computer," says Anna, "is there food on board?"

We could squirt some chocolate into Professor Bone's mouth.

Is that a joke?

If so, it's in the best possible taste!

Which part of the mouth is used for tasting?

Hugh pushes a button, and the ship jettisons its emergency candy supply. "It's working!" cries Anna, as the tongue starts pushing them backward. Up ahead they can see the foodpipe. But then everything stops. "What happened?" asks Hugh. "Why isn't he swallowing us?"

What has to happen to make Professor Bone swallow them?

Anna guides the Microship forward until its nose touches the top of the throat. Suddenly, flaps close off the windpipe, and the Microship goes tumbling into the esophagus.

After a short ride, they arrive in a big, dark cave with wrinkled walls—the stomach!

We just needed to touch the top of the throat. Easy!

What liquid is being produced by the stomach? Is it dangerous?

What is that liquid? Will it harm us?

I don't think I have the stomach for this!

Bad news! The chocolate has made Professor Bone hungry, and he's grabbed a snack! An avalanche of cake pours down the esophagus. The stomach stretches to make room, and its walls start spraying liquid onto the cake.

Anna quickly activates a shield to protect the Microship from the powerful acid.

After about an hour, the cake has turned to a soft, soupy mush. A ring of muscle below them opens and they enter the long, narrow tube of the small intestine.

Anna catches a glimpse of the SickBot. It spots her too—and vanishes deeper into the tube!

"I wonder what it was doing?" Hugh says.

"Look," says Anna, "the walls of the intestine are being damaged by stomach acid. We have to try to help!"

The SickBot is doing something to the intestine walls.

What normally protects the intestine walls from stomach acid?

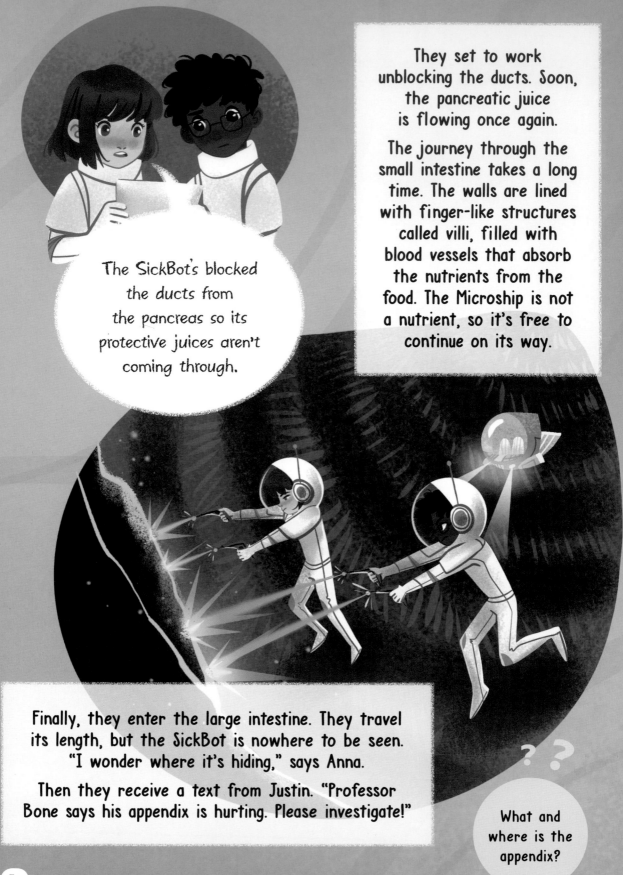

They set to work unblocking the ducts. Soon, the pancreatic juice is flowing once again.

The journey through the small intestine takes a long time. The walls are lined with finger-like structures called villi, filled with blood vessels that absorb the nutrients from the food. The Microship is not a nutrient, so it's free to continue on its way.

The SickBot's blocked the ducts from the pancreas so its protective juices aren't coming through.

Finally, they enter the large intestine. They travel its length, but the SickBot is nowhere to be seen. "I wonder where it's hiding," says Anna.

Then they receive a text from Justin. "Professor Bone says his appendix is hurting. Please investigate!"

What and where is the appendix?

Anna and Hugh locate the appendix and quickly travel there.

"There's the SickBot!" says Anna.

The evil robot is sending out bad germs into the appendix, making it swell up. It looks painful for poor old Professor Bone!

Anna blocks up the entrance of the appendix with the Microship, so the SickBot can't escape. Then they put on their diving helmets and swim down to the SickBot. Hugh distracts it while Anna finds the power switch, and switches it off.

Back aboard the Microship, they call Justin.

"Well done!" he says. "You've disabled the SickBot. However, the appendix is infected with germs that could spread to the rest of the body."

Anna has an idea. "Could the appendix be removed?"

Radical times cause for radical solutions!

Is the appendix important?

Luckily, the appendix is not an important organ and it can be removed! Justin Jectem uses his surgical skills to operate on Professor Bone, removing his appendix, along with the Microship and the SickBot. "We did it!"

The following day, Belinda Blood makes a video call to Anna, Hugh and Justin. "By now, Professor Bone must be extremely sick!" she cackles. "With him gone, I'll take all the credit for his invention, the Microship! I'll be the world's most famous scientist!"

Just then, Professor Bone enters the room. "Sorry, Belinda," he says, "I'm actually feeling extremely well! Your plan was foiled, thanks to Anna, Hugh, Justin, … and my amazing Microship!"

CHAPTER 2
AGENTS OF
N.R.G.

Ada, Isaac, and their robot pal Buzz are agents of the National Rescue Group (N.R.G). Normally, they are out and about fighting crime in Zap City. However, today there is a crisis! Someone has stolen all their special crime-fighting equipment. What's more, a villain has threatened the city with a massive power outage. Could the two things be linked?

We're ready for action, Madam Mayor!

Never fear!

We'll solve this crisis—even without our equipment.

Zap City's mayor, Connie Ductor, has summoned them to her office. "Evil billionaire Alec Trick has sent me a message," explains Connie. "Tonight, he's going to cut the city's power supply. The only place in Zap City left with electricity will be his hotel, Power Palace. He wants us all to use his power supply—and pay him for the privilege!"

We'd better remind ourselves about electricity. Here are all my files on the subject ...

DATA BLAST

ELECTRICITY is a form of energy. It is caused by tiny particles called electrons found in all matter. Each electron carries a small negative charge. We see electricity in nature in bolts of lightning. We harness electricity and use it to power appliances in our homes and businesses.

Rubbing a balloon against your sweater creates STATIC ELECTRICITY. It rubs negatively charged electrons from your sweater, making it positively charged. The balloon becomes negatively charged. Opposite charges attract, so the balloon sticks to your sweater. A negatively charged balloon can also attract very light objects such as paper.

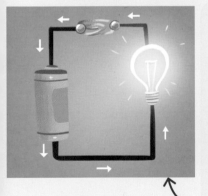

An ELECTRIC CURRENT is the flow of electrons in a closed loop, or circuit. A circuit can be used to power a device connected to it, such as a lamp. If you break the circuit, for example with a switch, the electricity stops flowing.

A BATTERY, or cell, is a power source for a circuit. The circuit needs a power source to push the electrons along. The more cells there are in a circuit, the stronger the power. Inside a battery, electrons travel from a starting point called the negative electrode to an end point called the positive electrode, through a chemical called an electrolyte. You can make a simple battery with a lemon, copper coin, and zinc nail! The lemon acts as the electrolyte, while the nail and coin are the electrodes.

A CONDUCTOR is a material through which electricity flows freely. Metals are conductors, and some conduct better than others. For example, copper is a better conductor than steel. An INSULATOR is a material that does not allow electricity to flow freely. Plastic is an insulator.

INSULATED COPPER WIRE   METAL FOIL CONDUCTS

Ada, Isaac, and Buzz decide to visit Power Palace. The door is locked. Suddenly, Alec Trick appears. The friends hide and watch as Alec opens the door by punching a code into a keypad. "He even dresses like a supervillain!" says Isaac. As the door closes behind him, they see a piece of paper fall from his pocket. Is it a clue?

There's a gap under the door, but I can't reach the note.

Neither can I!

"The static charge on the balloon will help us," Ada explains.

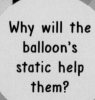

Why will the balloon's static help them?

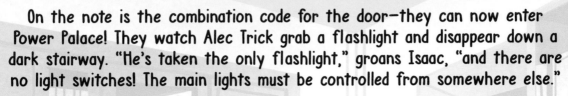

On the note is the combination code for the door—they can now enter Power Palace! They watch Alec Trick grab a flashlight and disappear down a dark stairway. "He's taken the only flashlight," groans Isaac, "and there are no light switches! The main lights must be controlled from somewhere else."

"Don't worry," says Ada. "We can make a flashlight of our own."

They are in a storage room full of supplies. They find a cardboard tube, a lightbulb, and a plastic cup for the body of their flashlight. Now they must build an electric circuit.

The friends find some copper wire and steel wire in the cupboards. Which would be best for their electric circuit?

Buzz cuts two lengths of the chosen wire.

Isaac wraps one end of each wire to the base of the bulb.

Ada joins the wires to the battery and the light comes on. "Right, we've got a circuit. Now we need to transfer it into the tube."

Nothing!

Why isn't it working?

Look at the picture. What's gone wrong?

They open up the tube and repair the circuit. Finally, they get the flashlight working.

It's live!

Ten seconds later, they hear a computer voice. It shouts: "Unauthorized light! Calling security!"

Buzz quickly cuts the wire on the flashlight, breaking the circuit. The light goes out.

So is that computer.

"False alarm," says the computer calmly.

"I think there was a time delay on that sensor," says Isaac. "Let's add a switch to our flashlight when we repair the circuit. That way, we can turn it off before 10 seconds pass, and avoid sounding the alarm."

"Look here," says Buzz. "I've found just what we need."

? ? ?

What items in the drawer will they use to make the switch?

As Isaac makes the switch, Ada puts some supplies in a bag—a spare bulb, a zinc nail, more wires, a copper coin, and two batteries. "Done!" cries Isaac. The three of them race through the door. After a long walk down a dark tunnel, they come to an underground room—Alec Trick's secret lair!

Let's check that computer for evidence!

Ada searches on the computer, while Isaac looks through the files. Buzz creates an alarm system, making a circuit that powers a buzzer rather than a lamp. He places his circuit under a mat. The weight of someone's foot on the mat will activate the switch and set off the alarm. Buzz tests it out, but the buzzer is too quiet.

How could Buzz make the alarm louder?

Buzz perfects his alarm and places it in the corridor they came down. If they hear it make a noise, there's another door they can escape through. "Check out these plans!" says Isaac, suddenly. "Trick has been meddling with the power station on Lake Volta, just north of Faraday Forest."

Ha ha ha!

Suddenly, the alarm goes off! They try to escape but discover both exits are blocked. Alec Trick grins evilly as he enters the room: "Welcome, agents of N.R.G. You fell into my little trap! My assistant, Dinah Mo, will escort you to your cell."

In the cell, Dinah Mo takes all their batteries—including the one in Buzz! She leaves the room, locking the door behind her. Disaster!

How can Ada and Isaac rescue Buzz, using things they find in the cell and Ada's bag?

? **?** 41

Ada and Isaac manage to build a new battery and get Buzz working again. With their robot friend's help, they escape the cell.

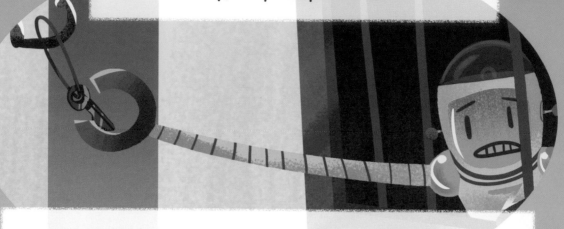

As the trio rush out of Power Palace, they can hear Alec Trick's voice … "I'm coming after you with my super-powerful magnet gun!" Alec Trick's warning blares out the loudspeaker.

Ada, Isaac, and Buzz head toward Zap City Park, where they stop for breath.

You won't escape me!

Buzz is worried. "A magnet gun sounds scary, especially for metal people like me!"

"Let's remind ourselves about magnetism, so we can be prepared," suggests Ada.

MAGNETISM is a force that certain objects have, which can attract (pull closer) or repel (push away) other objects. Magnetic objects contain metal, such as iron or steel. The area around a magnet affected by magnetic force is called its magnetic field.

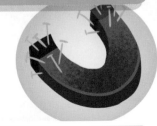

Here is some information I found about magnetism.

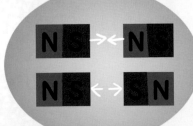

<u>POLES</u> are found at the ends of all magnets. They have a north pole and a south pole. The north pole of one magnet attracts the south pole of another, but the same poles repel each other.

Stroking a non-magnetic piece of metal, such as a needle, with a magnet makes tiny particles inside it align. This creates a temporary magnet.

Hitting a magnet with a hammer, or heating it up, breaks up the alignment of its particles, weakening or destroying its magnetism.

<u>MAGNETISM</u> can pass through some materials more easily than others. For example, it can pass easily through glass, plastic, paper, and wood, but only weakly through metal.

The Earth is full of metal, which makes it a giant magnet, with a north and south pole. When a small magnet is allowed to swing freely, its north pole will point roughly toward the Earth's north pole. This is how a compass is made. To make one, first magnetize a needle, then stick it through something that floats, such as a cork. Place it in a dish of water. The needle will turn and point north.

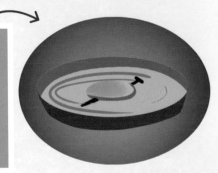

Ada, Isaac, and Buzz are on the run, with Alec Trick and Dinah Mo in hot pursuit!

You can't resist my magnetic attraction!

They stop in a quiet alleyway to catch their breath. "They're not far behind," says Buzz. "I can hear them coming!"

"Let's hide!" suggests Isaac. "Should we try the shack or the car?"

"Somewhere that the magnet gun can't easily penetrate," suggests Ada.

Where would be a good place to hide from the magnet gun? A metal car, or a wooden shack?

"Let's hide in the shack," says Ada. Then Alec Trick and Dinah Mo appear. Alec Trick fires his magnet gun at the shack.

"That magnet is strong," cries Ada. "This shack's walls may be wood, but the magnetic force can still get through. What should we do?"

"We must weaken the magnet's power. There must be something in here we can use," suggests Isaac, frantically looking around.

HELP!

?

What could they use in the shed to weaken the magnet's power and free Buzz?

Isaac charges out and bashes the magnet, so it loses its power and releases Buzz. "Run!" cries Ada. They sprint down the alleyway. Growling with frustration, Alec and Dinah chase after them.

The N.R.G. agents come to a busy street. Isaac pauses. "I've got an idea," he says. "Meet you two in Faraday Forest in half an hour."

Half an hour later, Ada and Buzz arrive at the meeting place. Isaac is waiting with a magnet Dinah Mo dropped. "I doubled back and grabbed it," he explains. "It must be a spare. We can use it against them."

"How?" groans Buzz, backing off. "They're not metal like me."

"No, but we could use it to defend ourselves," says Ada. "Magnets can repel other magnets, remember?"

Which poles of a magnet will repel each other? Which will attract?

Suddenly, Alec and Dinah appear. Dinah fires the Magnet gun.

Ada grabs the magnet from Isaac and points it at the one coming toward them. It works! The missile is repelled. It flies off and gets snagged on a tree branch. Alec and Dinah have now lost both their magnets. They are furious!

"We'll get you for this, Agents of N.R.G.!" screams Alec, as they slink away.

After Alec and Dinah have left, Ada, Isaac, and Buzz rest up and decide what to do next. "We need to get to Lake Volta, to the north, so we can find the source of Alec Trick's power."

"We can build a magnetic compass to find the way," suggests Ada.

How can they use the objects around them to build a magnetic compass?

Which way?

The trio make their way north to Lake Volta. There, they find an enormous power station.

"I remember from the plans that there's a door on the roof," says Isaac. "We could use the crane to get in." In the driver's cab, Buzz finds a remote control that raises the hook. But Buzz groans: "I'm worried about falling. If only we'd taken one of those magnets with us, it could hold me up and I'd feel safe."

Ada thinks for a moment. "Maybe we can turn the crane's iron hook into a magnet!"

POWER HOUSE

Do you know how to make an electromagnet? If not, read the next page!

Electricity and magnetism are both part of a force called **ELECTROMAGNETISM**. Pass electricity through a coil of wire wrapped around an iron bar and we make a temporary magnet, called an electromagnet. Switch off the current and its magnetism stops. We can strengthen an electromagnet by raising the electrical power, or by increasing the number of coils of wire around the bar.

Here is some information I found that might help us make a magnet using electricity.

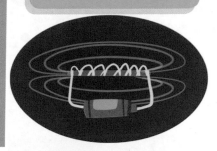

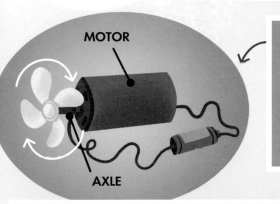

MOTOR

AXLE

<u>AN ELECTRIC MOTOR</u> is a device that converts electricity into mechanical energy, and it works thanks to electromagnetism. Within the device, an electric current flows through a wire loop held between the poles of a permanent magnet. The magnet and another mechanism in the motor makes the wire spin. This rotation can turn an axle and be used to drive machines.

<u>AN ELECTRIC BELL</u> works using electromagnetism. Pressing the bell button switches an electromagnet on. This pulls a clapper on a flexible strip toward it, which strikes a bell, but breaks the circuit and turns off the electromagnet. The clapper instantly springs back, turns on the circuit and the whole thing happens again. This repeats endlessly while the bell button is pressed.

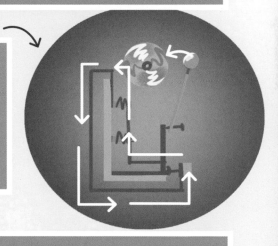

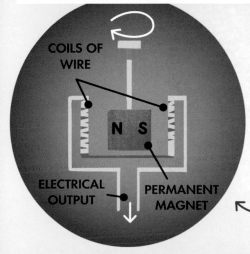

COILS OF WIRE

N S

ELECTRICAL OUTPUT

PERMANENT MAGNET

<u>A DYNAMO</u> generates electricity from magnetism. If you place a metal wire within the magnetic field of a permanent magnet and then rotate either the wire or the magnet, electricity flows through the wire. Some bicycle lights work this way. A dynamo is connected to a wheel. When the wheel spins, it causes the dynamo's magnet to rotate, generating electricity in the coil to power a light.

"We can wrap some copper wire around the crane's hook," says Ada, "but we need something to provide an electric current."

"We could use this," says Isaac, taking a battery from his pocket. "I grabbed it on the way to the forest—I was sure it would come in useful!"

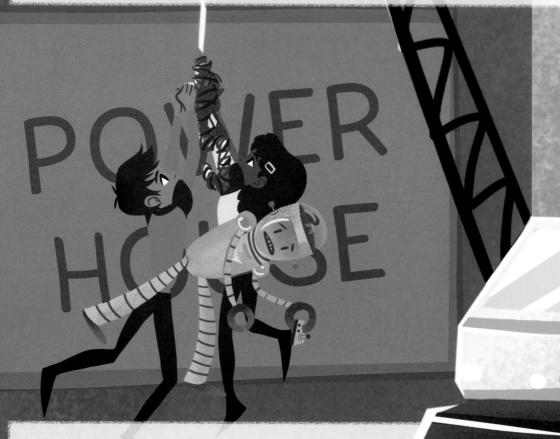

They still have some copper wire, which they wind around the hook, then connect it to the battery. Ada takes a deep breath and switches it on.

It works! But the electromagnet is very weak. It only lifts Buzz a little way off the ground.

"How can we increase the power?" asks Isaac.

"We can strengthen the electric current by adding another battery," suggests Ada.

"But we only have one battery," sighs Buzz.

What other way can they increase the power of the electromagnet?

They add some wire coils to their electromagnet, strengthening it enough to raise themselves over the flat roof. Then Isaac switches off the power to the electromagnet. The three of them drop down by the door leading into the building. It's bolted from the inside but they spot a small window above.

We won't get through that.

Suddenly, a drone flies up. Alec Trick's smirking face is on the screen. "Shocked you!" it laughs. Buzz uses the remote to swing the crane's arm around, crashing it into the drone. Ada picks up the pieces. "Hey, if we get this working again, it could fit through the window. We could use it to open the door! There's a battery here, but we need the right part to make the rotors turn."

Can you find the part that has fallen out of the drone? What is it?

They manage to fix the drone and adapt the crane's remote control to use with it. Buzz flies the drone through the window and tries to open the door from the inside. Meanwhile, a helicopter swoops in from above. Inside are two familiar faces ...

We must stop them!

Just as the helicopter touches down, Buzz manages to get the drone to slip the bolt. Buzz, Ada, and Isaac rush into the building. They hurry down a long staircase that leads to a large hall. Above them come Alec and Dinah's pounding footsteps. The trio hide out in an empty cafeteria.

"We need to get to the control room," says Isaac.

"We can create a distraction with this alarm," suggests Ada. But it does not work. They have to fix it. There's a part missing.

What is missing from the alarm's mechanism? Can you find the missing part on this page?

They manage to get the bell to work. "Get ready everybody!" says Ada, and she presses the button. The bell sounds. A few seconds later, Alec and Dinah burst through the door. Ada, Isaac, and Buzz are ready beside it and quickly run out. They close and lock the door behind them, trapping the evil pair inside the cafeteria.

HURRY!

What's inside the charger box? Solve the anagram MONDAY to answer.

The trio know they need to alert the mayor—fast! They find a phone but its battery is flat. Then Isaac spots a small box with a handle. It's a hand crank mobile charger.

"I've not seen one of these before," says Buzz.

"Clever, isn't it?" says Isaac. "You just turn the crank to charge the phone."

53

Isaac powers up the phone while Ada calls the mayor. "Alec Trick has taken over the Zap City Power Plant. We've trapped him and his assistant Dinah, but not for long. You need to send the police to arrest them!"

But the mayor has bad news: "I'm sorry, Ada. That billionaire bully has drained Zap City of all its power ... and all the police cars here run on electricity. They have no charge! We're literally powerless to help you until you get the hydroelectric plant working again."

Here is some information about hydroelectric power. It might help us.

HYDROELECTRIC POWER converts the energy of flowing water into electricity. First of all, engineers build a dam on a river that has a drop in height, or between two lakes at different levels. Near the bottom of the dam is a hole through which water from the higher level can flow. The water flows downhill through a channel to a turbine, which is like a large propeller. The flowing water turns the turbine.

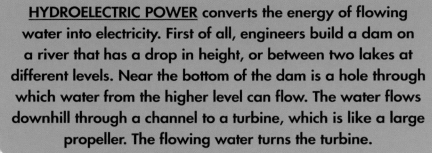

AN ELECTRICITY GENERATOR connects with the turbine's rotating shaft. This works just like a giant dynamo. Inside the generator, the shaft rotates a coil of copper wire at high speed within the magnetic field of powerful permanent magnets, creating an electric current in the coil.

DEMAND FOR ELECTRICITY CHANGES THROUGH THE DAY.

We need it less during the night than during the day, for example. At times of low demand, the electric generators and the turbines go into reverse, pumping water up into a pumped storage reservoir at a higher elevation.

At times of peak demand, the water is then allowed to flow back down through the turbines.

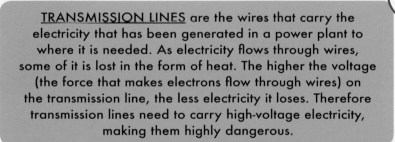

TRANSMISSION LINES are the wires that carry the electricity that has been generated in a power plant to where it is needed. As electricity flows through wires, some of it is lost in the form of heat. The higher the voltage (the force that makes electrons flow through wires) on the transmission line, the less electricity it loses. Therefore transmission lines need to carry high-voltage electricity, making them highly dangerous.

TRANSFORMERS are used to change the voltage of electricity. Power plants produce low-voltage electricity which needs to be upped by transformers to travel along the transmission lines. Homes and businesses need low-voltage electricity to power their devices. So more transformers, held in electricity substations and on poles, lower the voltage again.

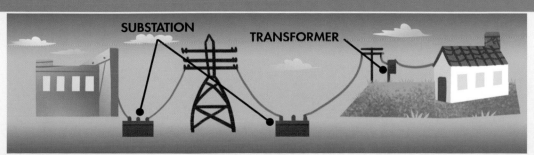

SUBSTATION TRANSFORMER

Isaac has been thinking. "Listen!" he says. "What can you hear?"

"Nothing!" says Buzz, straining his microphone ears.

No water, no power!

"Exactly!" says Isaac. "There's no sound. Why can't we hear the water rushing through the turbines below us?"

"You're right," says Ada pointing to the video screen in the control panels. "The turbines aren't turning. We need to find the water."

I	E	K	A	G	L	R	O	L	O	L	G
P	V	E	E	G	S	I	K	C	E	X	O
B	U	C	M	N	S	O	L	G	V	K	O
H	L	M	G	C	C	V	A	U	J	O	M
S	T	P	P	T	U	R	B	I	N	E	J
J	G	O	T	E	O	E	T	H	R	D	U
X	U	W	D	T	D	S	Z	X	I	C	S
C	U	E	S	Z	I	E	P	N	N	D	
U	E	R	U	Z	P	R	V	D	A	T	B
K	N	X	V	S	A	I	A	A	V	S	O
Z	K	V	T	W	M	M	R	F	U	J	R
T	Y	U	S	O	I	P	X	T	H	C	J

Ha! Now we've got them!

While the kids search for water, you should search for these words! Reservoir, turbine, storage, power, pumped, and dam. They may be diagonal or even backward.

56

Isaac and Ada find the water. Someone has closed the sluice gates and the reservoir is full to overflowing. Ada calls Buzz. "You need to open the sluices!" He pulls a lever, and the turbines start to turn. The power is back!

Release the reserve!

Doing it now!

How do the turning turbines generate electricity?

Ada and Isaac go back to the control room to find Buzz ... but Alec Trick and Dinah Mo have beaten them to it! Dinah's grabbed their robot pal.

"Thank you, Agents of N.R.G. You have done my job for me," gloats Alec. "As we speak, power from this plant is flowing toward my hotel, Power Palace."

This should shock you!

All power to me!

Buzz breaks free, and Ada, Isaac, and Buzz run as fast as they can out of the plant.

"Look!" says Buzz. "Alec Trick has connected the transmission line to a different set of pylons, cutting off Zap City and lighting up Power Palace."

"We'll have to turn off the electricity again to change them back," Isaac reminds them. "We can't touch live cables."

There's a small building nearby linked to the power plant's substation. Inside they manage to switch off the power. Then they go to reconnect the transmission lines so they take electricity to Zap City. But it's tricky, and the wires get all tangled up.

Looks like a case of crossed wires!

Can you find the far ends of cables A, B, C, and D to help the Agents of N.R.G. reconnect them? Which one comes out closest to the pylon?

A
B
C
D

They fix the transmission lines and race back to the substation building to switch on the power.

Powerful stuff!

As Ada pulls the lever, Alec Trick and Dinah Mo rush in. But this time the Agents of N.R.G. are ready. They tie the villains up with some spare cable and head for Zap City.

Ada phones the Mayor to tell her the good news. But the Mayor is not happy: "It's going crazy here. Everything's exploding. Alec Trick must have had one last trick up his sleeve."

Ada groans: "Oh no, I know what he's done. Quick, we must follow the transmission lines to town and get the voltage back down again."

Sparks are flying!

What has Alec Trick done? Where will the transmission lines take the trio?

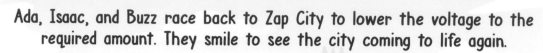

Ada, Isaac, and Buzz race back to Zap City to lower the voltage to the required amount. They smile to see the city coming to life again.

Later that day, in Zap City Plaza, they are awarded medals by Mayor Connie. "We want to thank you, Ada, Isaac, and Buzz," says the mayor, "for putting the zap back into Zap City!"

Just then, a police helicopter lands in the plaza. Out step the villains Alec Trick and Dinah Mo, who are about to be escorted to the town prison.

"Some time behind bars should do them a power of good!" smiles the mayor.

"What's happened to Power Palace?" asks Ada.

"Permanently unplugged!" the mayor replies.

CHAPTER 3
SPACE QUEST

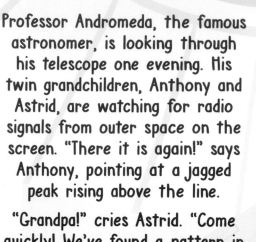

Professor Andromeda, the famous astronomer, is looking through his telescope one evening. His twin grandchildren, Anthony and Astrid, are watching for radio signals from outer space on the screen. "There it is again!" says Anthony, pointing at a jagged peak rising above the line.

"Grandpa!" cries Astrid. "Come quickly! We've found a pattern in the signals. Is this evidence of extraterrestrial life?"

The Professor joins them at the screen, as Apollo the dog barks excitedly. "I believe it is," he confirms, "and an intelligent one. What's more, it is coming from the Moon!"

"Can we send a message back?" asks Anthony.

"We can do even better than that," grins the Professor. "I've always wanted to go to the Moon. Let's build a rocket and meet this visitor in person!"

WOOF! WOOF!

Time for a
DATA BLAST!

ROCKET DESIGN In order to escape Earth's atmosphere, a rocket must overcome two major forces: gravity and air resistance. Gravity gives the rocket its "weight" and air resistance gives the rocket "drag." To counteract weight and drag, a rocket must have plenty of thrust (propulsive force). The greater the thrust, the faster the rocket goes.

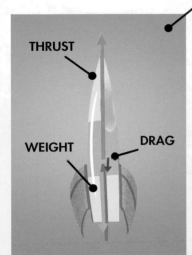

THRUST

WEIGHT   DRAG

TO MINIMIZE DRAG, the rocket's nose cone needs to be narrow and sharp, so it pushes air aside. The rocket's body should be narrow, so air flows smoothly over its length. To keep it stable in the air, the rocket needs fins at its base, much as an arrow needs feathers. But if these are too big, it will increase drag. You can increase a rocket's stability by adding mass to its nose cone.

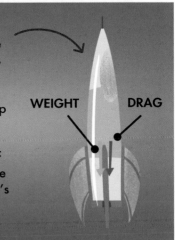

WEIGHT   DRAG

A ROCKET ENGINE burns its fuel inside a combustion chamber, blasting out gas and flames under great pressure through the rocket's base. This gives the rocket its thrust.

The fuel works with an oxidizer (something to react with the fuel) so it burns. Together, they are known as the propellant.

Propellants can be either solid or liquid. In solid-fuel engines, fuel and oxidizer are already mixed together as a solid. In liquid-fuel engines, the fuel and oxidizer are stored separately and then pumped into the combustion chamber to react. This allows the thrust to be controlled.

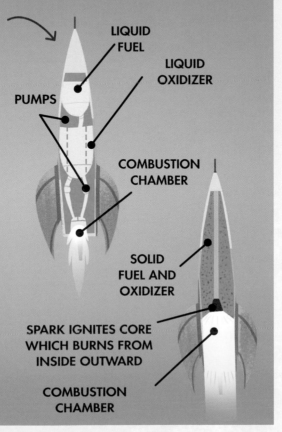

LIQUID FUEL

LIQUID OXIDIZER

PUMPS

COMBUSTION CHAMBER

SOLID FUEL AND OXIDIZER

SPARK IGNITES CORE WHICH BURNS FROM INSIDE OUTWARD

COMBUSTION CHAMBER

GRAVITY exerts a force on the human body. We don't feel it, because we're used to it. But this "g-force" gets as much as 3 times stronger in an accelerating rocket. This gives astronauts "tunnel vision" (they lose the edges of their vision) and they feel sleepy. To fight this, they need to tense up the body, and breathe in short bursts, or they may lose consciousness.

63

"We'll start with a model rocket," says Professor Andromeda. "If that goes well, we can scale up to the real thing. Anthony, you work on the body, and Astrid, you design the engine. I'll do some important thinking."

Anthony gives the rocket a super-sharp nose cone, and places three fins on its tail. Astrid designs the engine. She uses a solid-fuel propellant.

Soon they attempt their first launch. The rocket flies up above a tall tree, then falls back into a fishpond. "Not quite the Moon," observes the Professor. "What do we need more of to break free of Earth's atmosphere?"

T	H	R	A	R	E	A	T	N	C	E	A
G	A	V	T	Y	I	W	I	G	Y	A	G
A	J	K	L	I	R	R	E	S	U	S	E
V	D	I	T	Y	A	H	N	I	M	B	C
T	R	U	S	Y	I	G	A	R	G	B	N
Q	A	N	C	E	A	I	L	M	Y	H	A
A	G	R	G	R	A	V	I	T	Y	I	T
I	F	H	J	K	L	S	A	H	E	A	S
W	I	E	R	I	O	L	K	R	L	A	I
R	A	I	V	G	D	R	A	U	H	R	S
U	A	S	R	M	G	T	A	S	I	K	E
D	M	A	G	J	S	I	T	T	N	E	R

Oomph?

Power?

Can you find the word the children need? Look out for these other force related words: gravity, drag, weight, air, resistance.

One sunny morning the team tries testing a better, more powerful rocket. The Professor starts the countdown. "3, 2, 1 ... " Suddenly, Apollo races up to the rocket and leaps on. The rocket fires into the sky, with the dog aboard.

Andromeda does some fast calculations. "With Apollo's weight we'll need an extra 150 Newtons of thrust to keep the rocket accelerating. Astrid, can you pump 25 percent more fuel into the combustion chamber?"

Astrid stares at him. "I'm sorry, I can't!"

What can Astrid change to have control of the rocket's thrust?

That rocket's rocking!

They watch as the rocket tumbles back down. Just as it's about to crash, Apollo leaps off, into Anthony's arms. He wags his tail!

Astrid goes to work making changes to the engine. Meanwhile, Anthony and the Professor repair the rocket's body and test it in a wind tunnel.

"The rocket's unstable," sighs Astrid. "It also needs to be more aerodynamic."

Anthony shows her his designs. "I've given it a sharp nose cone! What else can I do?"

Compare Anthony's rocket design with the ones on page 63. What else can Anthony do to make the rocket more aerodynamic and stable?

More weeks go by as the team construct an even bigger, better rocket. This new rocket is twice as tall as the Professor.

When the rocket launches, the noise is deafening. The launch area fills with smoke and flames as the enormous craft soars into the sky. But then it starts to slow down … "Pump in more fuel, Astrid!" cries the Professor.

"I am!" she yells. "It's at the maximum!" They watch in despair as the rocket, like the others before it, plummets to the ground.

We have lift off!

Cosmic!

What has Anthony made too big with this rocket?

"We got the body shape just right this time," says Anthony, "but there was still too much drag."

"Yes, I think you may have tried to make it a little *too* stable," comments the Professor kindly.

The team refuses to give up. This time, they build a full-size rocket, big enough for them to fly in. They call it the *Artemis*.

Anthony designs space suits for all of them to wear while on the Moon. Astrid and the Professor work on Life-Support Systems to carry on their backs, giving them oxygen and radio communicators.

After several months of preparation, the day finally comes when they are ready to launch. The Professor presses the ignition button. At first there's silence. Then a huge rumbling fills their ears. Shaking, the *Artemis* starts to rise.

Farewell Earth!

Blast off!

The ride gradually becomes smoother and quieter. But then the rocket starts to wobble.

"Not again!" groans Anthony. "Why is it still unstable?"

"We need to find something to increase the mass in the nose cone," says the Professor.

?

What could they move into the nose cone to make the *Artemis* more stable?

?

68

After stabilizing the *Artemis*, they continue their journey toward space.

"Before we can travel to the Moon, we must first go into orbit around the Earth," Professor Andromeda reminds them.

"And we need to be going 7.94 km per second to get into Earth's orbit," remembers Anthony. "We need more thrust, Astrid."

"Increasing thrust now," says Astrid, pushing a lever.

The astronauts feel the pressure on their bodies from the g-forces as the *Artemis* accelerates.

Feeling sleepy.

Losing vision.

What must the astronauts do now to stay safe?

The astronauts manage to remain conscious as the *Artemis* continues to thunder skyward. Eleven and a half minutes after launch, they achieve orbit. The engine stops and everything goes silent. Then they feel themselves rising from their seats …

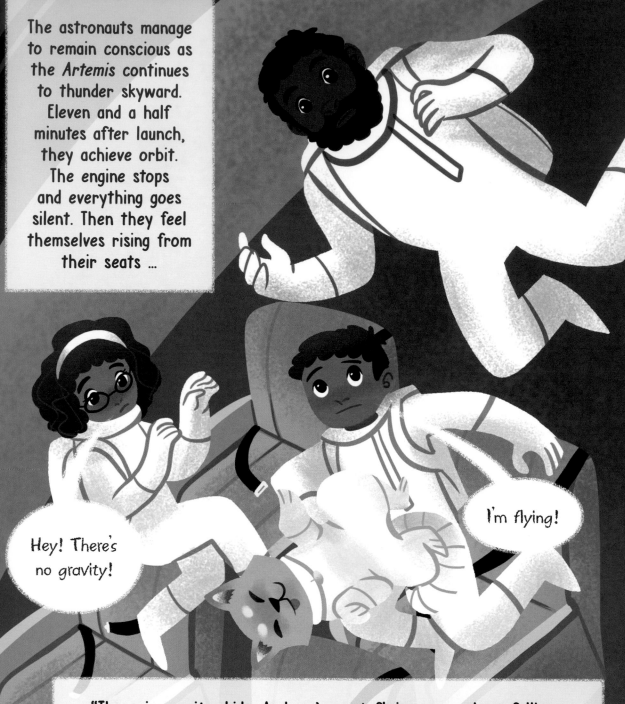

Hey! There's no gravity!

I'm flying!

"There is gravity, kids. And we're not flying so much as falling—toward Earth!" explains the Professor.

"Oh no! What went wrong this time?" says Anthony.

"Nothing went wrong," laughs his grandfather. "We're falling fast, but we'll never hit the Earth. The planet is curving away beneath us. You might say we're falling around it. In other words, we're in orbit!"

"I think it's time for another science lesson," says Astrid.

DATA BLAST

Here's what you need to know!

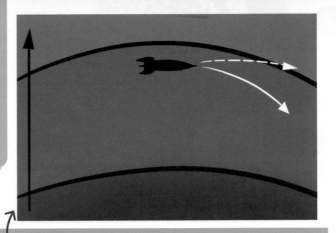

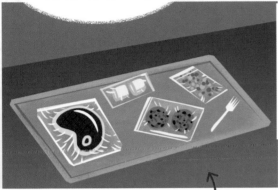

MOST SATELLITES are placed in "Low Earth Orbit," or LEO, 160–2,000 km (roughly 100 to 1,245 miles) above Earth. In LEO, atmospheric drag can slow a spacecraft down and it may fall back to Earth. Firing rocket boosters stops this by maintaining speed.

IN THE MICROGRAVITY of space, you will feel weightless. This can be fun, but also challenging. Food must be nibbled from packets or sucked through a straw. Muscles waste away in microgravity, so it's important to do regular exercise. When outside the spacecraft, you should use tethers (straps) to attach yourself to the vehicle, and keep from floating away! If you become detached, use the jet thruster on your spacesuit to fly back.

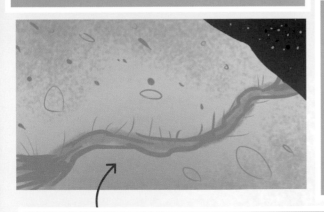

TO TRAVEL TO THE MOON from LEO, you must perform a "trans-lunar injection" (TLI). The rocket's engine moves the spacecraft from a circular orbit to an extremely elliptical (oval) orbit and takes it close to the Moon's orbit. The Moon's gravity will then draw the rocket in. When landing, use thrusters (small rocket engines) to control the speed. To calculate your altitude and speed, use radar—radio signals that are reflected off a surface to a receiver.

THE MOON has almost no atmosphere to protect it from the sun's radiation. The best way of surviving for any period would be to live inside a lava tube (a tunnel created by ancient volcanic lava). On the surface these look like long bulges. You can generate energy on the Moon by means of solar power. The best places to obtain this are certain mountains at the Moon's north pole, which have almost constant sunlight.

"What is our current altitude? And what's our speed?" the Professor asks.

"We're 200 km, or 124 miles, above Earth," reports Anthony.

"Our speed is 7.8 km per second," reports Astrid. "That's 4.8 miles per second!"

"Wait ... now we're 190 km above Earth," says Anthony, "which is to say, 118 miles."

"And our speed is 7.6 km per second," says Astrid, "so that's ... 4.7 miles per second."

What's happening? Unscramble these letters to find out what they need to do before it's too late. "FOOTSORE KRIB SECRET."

"We'll do two orbits of Earth, then head for the Moon," says the Professor.

"Look," says Anthony, "Space junk! Low Earth Orbit is full of it—the remains of old satellites and stuff jettisoned by space stations. Most are tiny, but when you're moving this fast, even they could cause damage."

From outside, they hear a soft crack. "Something's hit us!" cries Astrid.

For a moment, no one speaks. Then the Professor sighs: "We're okay, I think. It's time to start the trans-lunar injection, by changing our orbit."

What shape is the *Artemis*'s orbit now? What button should the Professor choose to change it to the right orbit?

Suddenly, the lights flicker out. "The ship's power comes from the solar panel," exclaims the Professor. "It must have been damaged by that space junk. Someone will have to go out and repair it."

After replacing the damaged solar panel with a new one, they prepare to go back inside. However, as Anthony and Astrid release their tethers, they somehow get tangled up ... and start floating away from the Artemis.

"Stay calm!" says Astrid. "If we can just untangle ourselves, we can use thrusters to get back to the rocket."

A few hours after they return from their spacewalk, the *Artemis* draws closer to the Moon.

"Time to prepare for landing," declares the Professor. "Strap yourselves in, crew! Apollo, that includes you. This could be bumpy!"

Astrid activates the thrusters to slow their descent to the lunar surface.

"What is our altitude and how fast are we moving?" asks the Professor.

What will Anthony use to answer the Professor? Lasers, radar, or thrusters?

"We should land on the Sea of Storms, where the signal came from," says the Professor.

"You want us to land in the middle of a stormy sea?" gulps Anthony.

"It's not a real sea," explains his grandfather. "It just looks like one from Earth. The Moon's 'seas' are dark because they're made of volcanic rock."

As the rocket begins to land, Andromeda is worried. "I don't understand," he says. "The signal came from there, but it's stopped and I can't see any sign of the alien. Why can't we see it?"

Can you spot where the alien might be living? What's it called?

They land on the dusty surface of the Moon. After putting on their spacesuits, they step out and start walking in long, bouncy strides toward the entrance to a cave.

"The Moon has one-sixth of Earth's gravity," the Professor explains through his two-way radio.

It's a giant leap!

For a dog as well as mankind.

The alien raises her hand in greeting. The human astronauts do the same. The alien points to her chest and says "Ah-Kee-Raa."

"Hello Akeera," says the Professor. He points to himself and says "Andromeda," then he introduces the others in turn.

Akeera points to a machine and shakes her head.

"That must be a communication device," says Astrid, "and the battery's dead. That's why we stopped receiving the signal! She's asking us to fix it. We can power it up with our solar panels—but we need constant sunlight."

Where on the Moon will they find constant sunlight?

The astronauts take Akeera back to the *Artemis*, then fly with her to a part of the Moon where there is constant sunlight. Here, they use the rocket's solar panel to charge her device. When it's working again, she points the device at Mars.

"Akeera must have friends there," Astrid realizes. "But I don't think they're answering."

"Can we take her to Mars to find them?" asks Anthony. "Do we have enough fuel?"

The Professor nods. "Yes! We can use solar power. Let's look at my Tourist's Guide to the Solar System to work out how to get there."

We'll be racing away from the Sun into the outer Solar System. The guide has lots of useful information.

MARS is the fourth planet from the Sun. Its reddish surface is covered in craters, valleys, mountains, and deserts. Watch for the volcano Olympus Mons. At three times the height of Everest, it is one of the tallest mountains in the Solar System! There is no liquid water on the surface of Mars but there is plenty of water ice at its poles and a lake of liquid water beneath the southern polar ice cap.

SUN   MERCURY   VENUS   EARTH   MARS

JUPITER is the fifth planet from the Sun and the largest in the Solar System. It is a "gas giant," which means it doesn't have a solid surface. Jupiter has a harsh, stormy atmosphere. It has 79 known moons, the largest of which is Ganymede. The fourth-biggest moon, Europa, has a water ice crust and a thin atmosphere composed mostly of oxygen. It has the smoothest surface of any object in the Solar System.

SATURN is the sixth planet from the Sun and another gas giant. It is famous for its rings, made up mostly of ice and dust. It has at least 62 moons, the largest of which is Titan. Another of Saturn's moons, Enceladus, is covered in clean, fresh ice, making it one of the most reflective bodies in the Solar System, but also very cold. It's famous for the giant jets of water shooting out of its south pole.

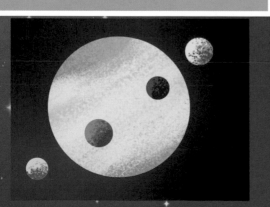

Running <u>LOW ON OXYGEN?</u> You can generate it from water by a process called electrolysis—an electric current passed through the water separates it into two gases, hydrogen and oxygen.

Running <u>LOW ON FUEL?</u> Try gravity assist! You can use the gravity of a planet to boost the speed and power of your spacecraft as you fly past it.

Want to <u>GROW FOOD IN SPACE?</u> As there's no gravity, roots grow in all directions, and water and nutrients float. You need to glue plant seeds to little bags filled with soil and fertilizer. The bags should be made of material that absorbs water. LED lights will give the plants the energy they need to grow.

<u>THE ASTEROID BELT</u> lies between the orbits of Mars and Jupiter. It is a region populated by a vast number of odd-shaped bodies called asteroids, ranging in size from dwarf planets to specks of dust. Even the smallest asteroid could cause huge damage if it hits you at 25 km per second (15.5 miles per second)—their average speed.

<u>WHEN YOU RETURN TO EARTH</u>, take care. Hitting the air particles at the top of the atmosphere will cause friction. This produces intense heat. To avoid burning up, approach it with a blunt surface first—the side of the rocket rather than the nose cone. The blunt shape creates a shock wave, keeping the heat at a distance. It also creates more drag, slowing the craft's fall.

The journey to Mars takes more than eight months. During that time, the crew of the *Artemis* gets to know Akeera, and she learns a little English.

"That's Proxima Centauri, our closest star after the Sun," says Professor Andromeda. "Do you come from a planet circling it, Akeera?"

"Akeera come from planet Namaweyho," replies the alien. "Visit your Solar System on Namaweyho explorer vessel. Vessel visit moon of Earth and Akeera get off. Then Akeera get left behind."

As *Artemis* draws closer to Mars, Akeera gets more and more excited. "Vessel sending signal from high place on Mars," she says. "We must go high place."

Where on Mars do you think Akeera's vessel might be?

They land high up by the side of a large crater, and step out of the *Artemis*. "Signal come from inside crater!" cries Akeera, running to its edge.

But the explorer vessel isn't there. Instead she finds a radio device. She presses a button and listens to a message in her own language. Then she stops glowing. "Explorer vessel already gone," she says sadly. "Up there!"

"How far away is Jupiter?" asks Anthony.

"Around 550 million km ... or 341 million miles," replies the Professor, "It'll take us about a year and a half. We'll need more oxygen."

"We can make more from the water ice on Mars," says Astrid.

"I'll make sure we have enough food!" says Anthony.

What do they need from the supply room to make oxygen? What will they use for food?

On their way to Jupiter, Astrid has to navigate the asteroid belt. Anthony helps her using the ship's radar. They are nearly through the belt when he says: "Uh-oh! A car-sized object is flying straight at us. It's 500 km away—that's only 310 miles!"

How much time do they have to change course, assuming the asteroid is moving at average orbital velocity (25 km, or 15.5 miles, per second)?

Having made it through the asteroid belt, the *Artemis* begins to be drawn by the pull of Jupiter's gravity. "Message from explorer vessel," cries Akeera. "They go smooth place near Jupiter."

Where might Akeera's friends be found?

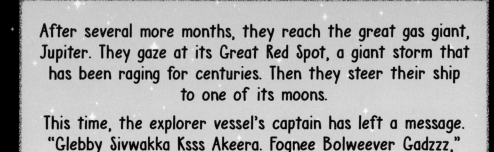

After several more months, they reach the great gas giant, Jupiter. They gaze at its Great Red Spot, a giant storm that has been raging for centuries. Then they steer their ship to one of its moons.

This time, the explorer vessel's captain has left a message. "Glebby Sivwakka Ksss Akeera. Fognee Bolweever Gadzzz," says his hologram.

"He say they wait for me here very long time," Akeera translates. "But finally they have to go ... go to place near ringed planet with big fountains."

The Professor hesitates. "That could take us another year to reach! But I've loved every minute of our voyage so far. What do you think, Astrid and Anthony?"

"Let's go for it!" they say.

What's he saying?

It's alien to me!

Where are they going?

It takes *Artemis* and its crew a year to reach Saturn. They explore its spectacular ring system. Finally, they visit the place with the "big fountains," and there, at last, they find the explorer vessel ... Akeera turns to Astrid, Anthony, the Professor, and Apollo. "Thank you for all you do for me! You have been most kind! I will miss you!"

We'll miss you too.

Safe journey.

WOOF!

After they have said farewell to her, they return to the *Artemis*. "At last," sighs the Professor. "Time to go home!"

"I'm afraid we're running low on fuel," points out Anthony.

"And the sun is too far away to give us much solar power," worries Astrid. "How are we going to get back?"

With their fuel running low, how can they get back to Earth?

Three years later, and six years since they began their epic journey, the astronauts arrive back near Earth ...

Home!

I'm spaced out!

WOOF!

No more space junk food!

But just as they approach the edge of Earth's atmosphere, things start going wrong. "It's getting dangerously hot!" cries Anthony. "The rocket can't take it!"

How should they turn the *Artemis* to save the rocket and themselves?
(a) 90 degrees
(b) 180 degrees
(c) 110 degrees.

The astronauts manage to enter Earth's atmosphere, and they land the *Artemis* in their back garden.

"I feel ten times heavier," says Astrid, as she steps down from the *Artemis*. "I'm not used to Earth gravity."

"Looks like Apollo's not used to it either!" says Anthony.

Akeera!

Glebby Sivwakka!

The family settles back in normal life. One day, they receive a message. "I can translate!" exclaims Astrid. "She says: 'Greetings.'" They all smile as Akeera continues in English. "I am back home now. Sending you my love from Namaweyho. I will never forget you."

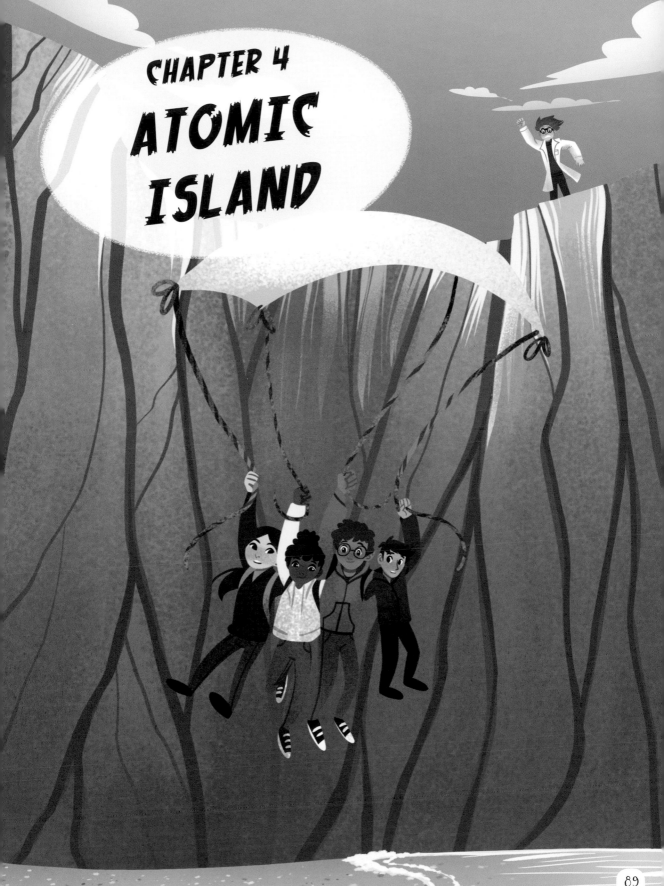

Molly Cool, Andy Matter, and Tess Tube volunteer at the Metro City Science Museum. One day, they spot a shattered glass cabinet.

"Something's been stolen!" cries Molly.

Molly

Tess

Andy

"Wait, there's a note," says Tess Tube. "It's from the thief."

Greetings FOOLS,

That's right! I have STOLEN your reversium, and KIDNAPPED the museum's curator! Ha, ha, ha. Reversium, as you know, is the only material that can make time go backward. Such a rare and interesting material deserves to be in the hands of a REAL scientist, not a bunch of AMATEURS. I have taken it to my secret laboratory on ATOMIC ISLAND. I will use it to hold the whole world to ransom!

Yours,

Dr. Adam Smasher

"We have stop Dr. Smasher!" says Molly.

"Wait," says Tess. "The burglar also seems to have dropped some pages from a science book. Perhaps they contain information that will help us?"

DATA BLAST

Check it out!

STEEL and TUNGSTEN are hard metals.

LEAD and COPPER are soft and easy to shape.

MATERIALS with different properties are useful for different tasks. Sometimes you might want a strong material—such as steel. Sometimes you might need something air can pass through—such as cloth. Sometimes you might want something that does not melt easily—such as Tungsten, which has a high melting point.

SILVER and GLASS are reflective.

GLASS and TUNGSTEN shatter easily.

When materials change, their properties change, too. Some changes can be reversed—for example, water can be frozen, and ice can be melted. Others are irreversible.

REVERSIBLE CHANGES

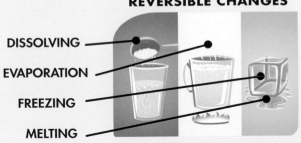

DISSOLVING
EVAPORATION
FREEZING
MELTING

IRREVERSIBLE CHANGES

COOKING FOOD
MIXING CONCRETE
BURNING WOOD

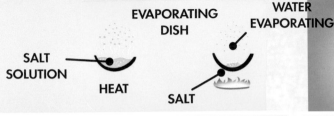

EVAPORATING DISH

WATER EVAPORATING

SALT SOLUTION

HEAT

SALT

HEAT ON THE MOVE

EXAMPLES OF REVERSIBLE CHANGES

• SALT dissolved in water forms a solution and can be separated through evaporation.
• WATER can be separated from a mixture through distillation. The water is heated and trapped as steam. When it cools, it turns back into liquid water.

CONDUCTING HEAT

Some materials are better at conducting (moving) heat than others.
• Metals are good CONDUCTORS.
• Materials that do not conduct heat well are known as INSULATORS. They include plastic, styrofoam, and glass.

Molly, Andy, and Tess set out on a boat for Atomic Island. But on the way, the boat gets tossed around on giant waves. Molly falls overboard! Hours later, she wakes up on a beach alone. She is surrounded by wreckage—is it from the boat?

This rock is sharp. Could I use it to write?

Molly decides to explore the island, but she wants to leave a message for her friends in case they show up while she's gone. She needs something to write on: a material with a smooth surface that's soft enough to scratch into, but not so soft the message could get washed away.

Which material should she choose to write a message on?

(a) Beach sand
(b) Copper saucepan
(d) Steel panel
(e) Plastic bottle

Near the beach, Molly finds a metal door that has rusted shut. She returns to the beach to find something that will help her open it. She's overjoyed to find her friends waiting for her there.

I found a lead pipe, wooden poles, and a tungsten bowl.

Great beach combing!

Tess and Andy show Molly a collection of objects they've managed to retrieve from the wreckage of their boat. "Tungsten is the hardest metal," says Andy. "If we bash that door with the tungsten bowl, might it open?"

I've got a steel rod, styrofoam, cloths and a roll of silver foil.

What might go wrong with tungsten? What could they use as an alternative?

Taking the materials with them, they break through the rusted metal door. Beyond the door, a staircase takes them down to an underground tunnel. The tunnel continues straight for a while, then bends sharply to the right. A sudden noise stops them in their tracks.

There's someone around that corner!

How can we see who it is?

On reflection, I have an idea...

Look back at what they found on page 93. Is there something reflective? How could they use it?

In the reflection, they see Dr. Adam Smasher coming toward them. They run fast in the other direction. They turn left, then right, then right again, then left again. It's like a maze! Soon, they are hopelessly lost.

Haven't we been down this tunnel before?

Can you trace a route to escape from the maze? The right route will spell the name of a soft metal.

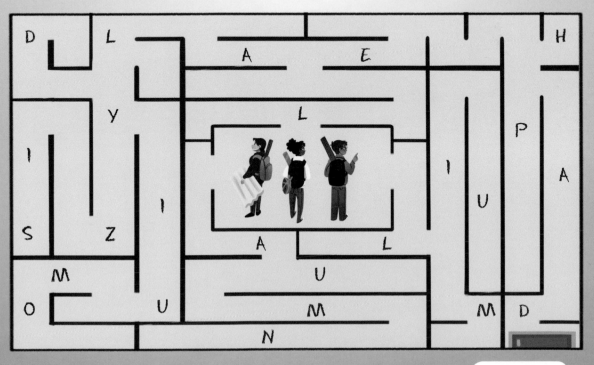

ESCAPE

The door from the maze leads into a live volcano! It's incredibly hot. They hear Dr. Smasher's voice over a loudspeaker. "Welcome to Atomic Island—the hottest place to be. I hope you like it here ... since you can never leave!"

You kids will rue the day you decided to meddle in MY plans!

It's hard to breathe!

I don't lava this!

The door back to the maze makes a click. "It's locked!" says Andy. The lava bubbles and smokes dangerously beneath them. It releases gases that make them choke.

What material can they use to protect themselves from fumes, while still being able to breathe?
(a) The tungsten bowl
(b) Silver foil
(c) Cloth

Molly, Adam, and Tess make themselves masks. Together they explore the volcano's interior, searching for an escape. They find the start of a tunnel, but it's blocked by a pair of steel doors.

They search for an object they can use to transport the super-hot lava to the doors. It needs to be made of a material with a very high melting point.

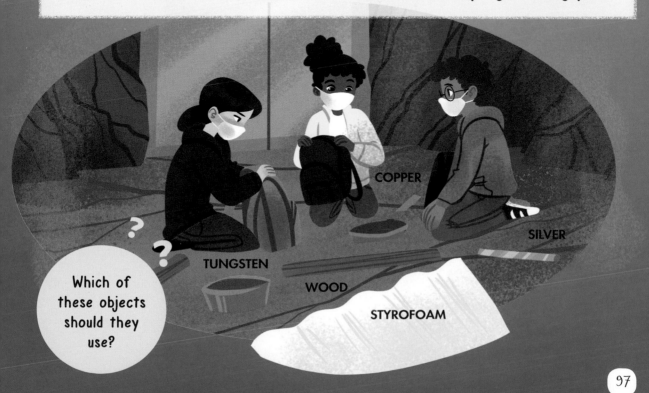

Molly, Andy, and Tess venture closer to the pool of lava. It is extremely hot and they start to sweat. Suddenly, the ground shakes and a huge red-hot fountain shoots into the air, landing close to their feet. They stagger backward in shock.

Once they've recovered, the trio continue toward the lava. Molly kneels down, preparing to scoop up some of the lava.

Wait! Is metal a conductor or insulator of heat?

That's the burning question.

Is metal a conductor or insulator of heat?

What material could Tess use as an insulator?

"If it's a conductor, then the heat will move from the lava through the metal to my hand," says Molly. "I could get burnt—unless I can find an insulator to put between the metal and my skin."

They melt the steel doors and break through to the tunnel beyond. After a short walk, they emerge by a lagoon. Beside it is a train track with a steam train on it. Standing on top is a ten-year-old boy!

It's me, Mike Slater, the museum curator!

Didn't you have a beard?

I thought your hair was white!

"Adam Smasher used the reversium to reverse time, and turn me into a kid!" says Mike. "I escaped from his laboratory in this train. I could take you back, but it's run out of fresh water for the boiler. The water in the lagoon is salty."

How can they make fresh water from the saltwater lagoon? The correct answer is hidden in his wordsearch. Also watch for the words "saltwater," "lagoon," and "separate."

X	U	O	E	O	G	X	G	D	N	R	A
A	A	P	A	X	L	U	R	I	U	M	S
R	P	S	S	R	R	N	G	S	K	S	K
G	A	D	T	E	X	I	O	T	G	E	E
P	S	P	U	T	P	P	S	I	A	G	O
O	E	R	E	A	D	A	X	L	D	C	O
A	R	E	D	W	R	S	R	L	E	X	R
G	P	G	A	T	E	E	E	A	Z	E	R
E	O	G	N	L	D	D	I	T	T	O	E
G	G	L	I	A	E	D	R	I	R	E	P
E	R	S	G	S	O	O	R	O	E	R	S
S	E	O	L	A	G	O	O	N	O	E	A

Molly, Andy, and Tess make fresh water, which they pour into the locomotive's boiler. Mike lights a fire, which heats the water to create steam. The steam builds up pressure in the engine, which drives the locomotive. Soon, they are puffing along the track.

And then, quite suddenly, it starts snowing!

A huge voice booms out from the mountain. "I know you've hijacked my train!" bellows Dr. Smasher. "However, thanks to my stolen reversium, I can rewind the weather to last winter ... and freeze the tracks!"

The train can't travel any further on these icy tracks.

We need to make salt to melt the ice.

Remember, the lagoon's water is salty.

What method can they use to extract the salt from saltwater? Work it out from this anagram —"AVIATOR OPEN."

The train chugs past a half-built railway station and stops in a tunnel. Mike points to a doorway ahead. "There's Smasher's underground lab," he says.

From behind them comes the sound of another approaching train. Dr. Smasher and his guards are coming after them!

Molly runs back to the half-built station. She picks up a bag of cement. "We can make concrete with this and pour it over the tracks," she says.

They mix the cement with water to make concrete and pour it over the tracks. "Hold on!" says Andy. "Can't Smasher just melt the concrete and turn it back into cement and water?"

Can concrete be turned back into cement and water?

After blocking up the tunnel, they enter Smasher's laboratory. It's freezing cold in there. They soon see why ... "Smasher's encased the reversium in a block of ice!" says Molly.

"Let's smash it to ice cubes," says Andy, attacking it with a hammer.

"It's too big," says Tess. "It'll take too long. We need to think of something else."

Then Molly has a spark of inspiration. "We could build a fire," she suggests.

What will happen if they heat it? Will it burn or melt? Will it turn into water or steam?

DATA BLAST

"The hot topic," says Tess, "is how do you build a fire? Let's find out."

THE FIRE TRIANGLE: OXYGEN + FUEL (MATERIAL CONTAINING CARBON) + HEAT = FIRE

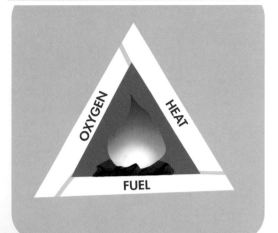

OXYGEN   HEAT

FUEL

Some materials, such as wood, burn because they contain the element carbon. When they are heated to a certain temperature, the carbon inside them reacts with oxygen in the air and they burst into flames. This is called their "combustion point." Because their combustion point is lower than their melting point, they burn rather than melt. All living matter, or matter that was once living, contains carbon.

VEGETABLES

CONCRETE

WOOL

COPPER

LEAVES

WOOD

COAL

What materials in this picture will burn?

Soon they've gathered lots of material in a big pile. They have their fuel. They have oxygen (in the air). Now all they need is heat to make a fire. Mike takes out a box of matches and prepares to set light to the pile.

"Wait!" says Molly. "We need to plan what we're going to do once the ice melts. How are we going to get the heavy block of reversium out of this underground lab and back home?"

"Let's see if there are any clues here," says Tess, taking out the torn pages they found in the museum.

Check it out!

DATA BLAST

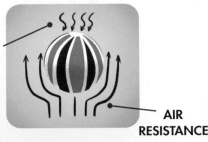

GRAVITY

AIR RESISTANCE

AIR PUMPED IN

FLOATING AND SINKING
If the density of an object is equal to or less than the density of the water it displaces (pushes aside), then the object will float. For example, most wood is less dense than water, so it floats. An object that is more dense than the water it displaces—such as a ship's anchor— will sink.

AIR AND WATER RESISTANCE
When objects travel through the air or water, they are slowed down by the tiny particles of gas or liquid. A thrown ball strikes air particles, which slow it down. In a similar way, swimmers are slowed down by water particles.

AIR PRESSURE
The air is always pushing against things. This is called air pressure. You can increase air pressure by pumping air into a closed space.

MACHINES are devices that make it easier (so less energy is needed) to move an object.

INCLINED PLANE
This is a flat surface with one end higher than the other. It allows heavy objects to be slid up to a higher point rather than be lifted.

WHEEL AND AXLE
This is a wheel with a rod attached to the middle, to help lift loads. The bigger the wheel, the more you have to turn it, but the less effort it takes.

PULLEY
This is made up of a wheel with a groove in it and a rope that fits into the groove. One end of the rope is attached to the load, and you pull the other.

LEVER
This long tool can help to lift or move an object. A long but relatively weak movement at one end can produce a small but forceful movement at the other end.

WEDGE
This has two surfaces at an angle to each other. It can be used to separate two objects, to keep things together, or to prevent movement.

Mike lights the fire, and soon it is burning nicely. Water starts to drip from the ice block. "When all that ice melts, it will create a lot of water," Tess points out.

"A little guy like me might drown," gasps Mike.

"We should try to find something to float on," says Molly.

I've got a sinking feeling.

What objects can they use to help them float when the water level rises?

The ice melts, and the water rises. The four of them cling to their floating objects. Eventually, the water washes into a drain in the floor, and the water level begins to drop. The reversium is now revealed in all its glory ...

It's amazing!

How will we get it out of here?

Outside the lab, they can hear Dr. Smasher shouting. He sounds furious!

"No pressure ... but he's here!" says Andy. "And we're trapped."

"We can escape through there," says Mike, pointing to a locked pair of doors, "if we can get the key out of this." He shows them a corked bottle.

Look, a pump! Do we need more or less pressure in the bottle?

Can you answer Tess's question?

They manage to get the key out of the bottle and open the doors. Parked in the tunnel beyond is a pickup truck.

"We can put the reversium on the back of the truck," says Mike.

"But how can we lift it on?" asks Andy.

"We could create a pulley," says Molly. "We can use one of the bike's wheels and the rope."

All pulley together!

It's still too heavy.

However hard they pull, they cannot lift the reversium. "Maybe we should add another machine to this one?" suggests Andy, eyeing the remaining bicycle wheel and the wooden pole.

What machine can they add to the pulley to help them lift the reversium?

The gang manages to lift the reversium onto the back of the pickup truck. They also take some equipment that might be useful. As they are packing the last of this, Dr. Smasher arrives with his guards.

Molly, Andy, Tess, and Mike make their escape. The tunnel spirals upward through the mountain. Eventually they emerge on a rocky slope high above the sea. Molly, Andy, and Tess get out to check everything is safe in the back. The slope is very steep, and the truck starts rolling slowly down it toward the edge of a cliff.

Just in time, they stop the truck, and Mike climbs out. However, the reversium and most of their equipment roll off the back! They watch in despair as the precious cargo plunges over the cliff and crashes onto the beach far below.

"We still have some equipment," says Andy, pointing to the rope and canvas sheets.

"We could use the canvas and rope to make a parachute," says Tess. "When we jump off the cliff with it, the parachute will create air resistance. It'll trap lots of air particles, slowing us down."

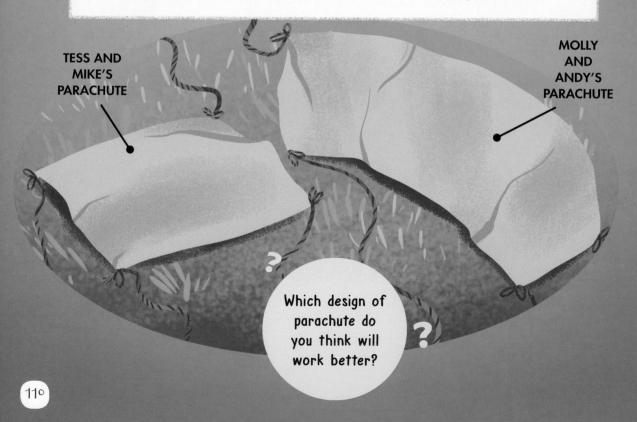

TESS AND MIKE'S PARACHUTE

MOLLY AND ANDY'S PARACHUTE

Which design of parachute do you think will work better?

The friends choose the right parachute, which takes them down slowly on to the beach. "Look!" Andy points out. "We can escape the island in that submarine."

"But how do we get there with the reversium?" asks Molly.

"We can use that boat," says Tess.

But the reversium is too heavy for them to lift into the boat. They look at the objects scattered on the beach. Is there anything that can help them get the reversium into the boat?

Which of these objects could help them move a heavy object to a higher point?

They manage to get the reversium into the boat. But then they discover the boat has no oars! "Maybe we can use the wooden poles as oars," says Andy.

They try using the poles, but they don't work very well.

This is oar-ful!

How are we supposed to row it?

"The poles don't cause much water resistance," says Tess.

"What do you mean?" asks Mike.

"I mean the water flows around them too easily because of their shape." (The diagram below shows what she's talking about!)

The kids decide they need to change the shape of the poles. Mike produces a penknife with a small saw. What object (shown on page 111) could be joined to the poles to improve their shape?

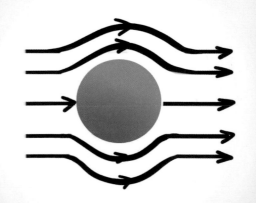

They manage to change the shape of the poles, making them work much better as oars. Soon, they arrive at the submarine and climb aboard. Unfortunately, the hatch is too small for the reversium to fit through it.

They tie the reversium to the sub's tower, then try opening the hatch. However, it becomes stuck. No matter how hard they pull, it won't open.

Eventually, they manage to open the hatch and climb inside the submarine.

"The ballast tank is the part of the submarine that makes it float or sink," says Tess. She checks her screen. "At the moment it's full of air."

Andy remembers their science lesson. "If the density of the submarine is equal to or less than the density of the displaced water, the object will float."

How do we make the submarine go down?

There has to be a way. Let me sink ...

How can they make the submarine sink?

They make the submarine sink, then set a course for home.

Suddenly, the door bursts open. They turn to see Dr. Smasher. "A-ha!" he cackles. "You didn't think it would be that easy to get away, did you? I suspected you would try to steal my submarine, so I stowed myself aboard!"

Now you're in deep water!

"I'm taking you and the reversium back to Atomic Island, where you will stay forever!" declares Dr. Smasher. He pulls a remote control from his pocket and uses it to turn the submarine.

"What now?" Andy groans to Molly. "Listen," she whispers. Andy hears the sounds of helicopters and police sirens, from far above them.

"They'll never catch me down here!" says Smasher. He walks over to the intercom. "Guards, come and tie up these interfering kids." Quick as a flash, Molly presses a button.

What has fast-thinking Molly done? What happens next?

When the submarine reaches the calm surface of the sea, Dr. Smasher realizes that the game is up. "Not the police! I have to get to the reversium. I'll use it to turn them all into babies!" He tries to rush out of the room, but bangs his head on the door, and knocks himself out.

A few days later, they meet at the science museum, where Andy shows them the reversium, back in its case. "I can't thank you enough!" he says. "I'm so glad you saved our best exhibit from being smashed. And I'll soon be back to my old self … no pun intended!"

"I doubt it could have been smashed anyway," says Molly. "It survived being packed in ice, falling off a cliff, and a journey under the sea. I think it might be unbreakable!"

"Just like our friendship!" smiles Tess.

ANSWERS

CHAPTER 1

PAGE 7

Blood in veins goes from the body's cells to the heart. The blood is under less pressure in veins than it is in arteries, so the walls don't have to be as strong as artery walls.

PAGE 9

Red blood cells carry oxygen in arteries from the heart and lungs to the body's cells.

Red blood cells carry carbon dioxide in veins from the cells back to the heart and lungs.

They should camouflage themselves as an antibody. Antibodies are disease-fighting proteins in the blood, so would not be attacked. Bacteria are foreign bodies that will be attacked by white blood cells.

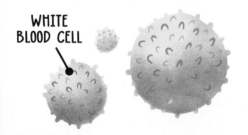

WHITE BLOOD CELL

PAGE 10

They are in a capillary. Capillaries are very fine networks of blood vessels that carry blood through the tissues of the body.

PAGE 11

They are in an artery. It does not lead to the heart. It carries blood away from the heart to the body's cells.

PAGE 12

The things within blood that help it clot are called platelets. They are very tiny fragments of cells.

PAGE 13

The mesh will turn into a protective scab.

PAGE 14

The heart has four chambers—the right atrium, the right ventricle, the left atrium, and the left ventricle.

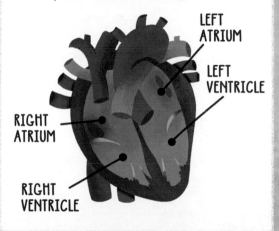

LEFT ATRIUM

LEFT VENTRICLE

RIGHT ATRIUM

RIGHT VENTRICLE

PAGE 15

The right ventricle of the heart leads to the pulmonary artery, which in turn leads to the lungs.

PAGE 18

Yes, they have reached the lungs. The chamber that keeps expanding and shrinking is an alveolus.

PAGE 19

Bright red blood cells are filled with oxygen. When the red blood cells have given up their oxygen to the body's cells, they turn a darker, brownish-red shade. So blood moving through the arteries is bright red, and blood moving through the veins is brownish-red.

A gas can move through the wall because its molecules are very small. The gas moving from the chamber (alveolus) into the capillary is oxygen. The other gas moving through the wall is carbon dioxide. It moves from the capillary into the alveolus.

PAGE 20

The tubes are called bronchioles. They eventually lead to the bronchi and the trachea or windpipe.

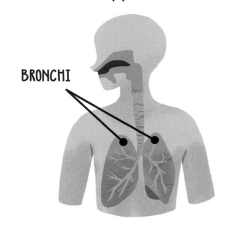

BRONCHI

PAGE 21

Yes, it's very important for Professor Bone to keep breathing. We need to breathe because our cells need oxygen to convert nutrients from our food into energy for our body. We also need to breathe to get rid of the waste gas, carbon dioxide.

PAGE 22

The hairs on the walls of the trachea are called cilia. They trap dust and other particles in the air that we breathe in. The body expels them by coughing. Anna and Hugh could free themselves by making the Prof cough.

PAGE 23

The "doors" are vocal cords. The sounds they are making are speech. When we speak, the vocal cords close to a narrow gap. The air moving through the gap makes the vocal cords vibrate, creating speech sounds. Anna and Hugh can get them to open by asking Professor Bone to stop speaking.

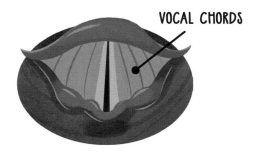

VOCAL CHORDS

PAGE 26

The tongue is used for tasting. Its top surface contains clusters of special taste-sensitive cells called taste buds. When food touches these, it sends signals to the brain. The brain interprets these (along with smell signals sent by the nose) and works out what is being tasted.

PAGE 27

Swallowing is triggered by food touching the top of the throat. The Nanoship has to touch the top of Professor Bone's throat before he can swallow them. When it touches the top of his throat, this will produce a reflex reaction, pushing the nanoship into the foodpipe.

PAGE 28

The liquid produced by the stomach is gastric juice. It contains a powerful acid to break down food and kill microorganisms, so it is dangerous to the Nanoship.

GASTRIC JUICES

PAGE 29

The intestine walls are protected from stomach acid by pancreatic juice.

PAGE 30

The appendix is a sac attached to the large intestine near where it joins with the small intestine.

PAGE 31

The appendix does not have any important digestive function. It can safely be removed.

CHAPTER 2

PAGE 36

By rubbing the balloon on her head, Ada is rubbing negatively charged electrons off her hair and onto the balloon. The balloon therefore becomes negatively charged. The negative charge in the balloon makes the electrons in the piece of paper move to the other side of their atoms (like charges repel, or push apart) and this makes the piece of paper positively charged. Because opposite charges attract, the paper will be attracted to the balloon.

PAGE 37

They should choose the copper wire, because copper is a better conductor of electricity than steel. This is because it contains a higher number of free electrons. Although silver is an even better conductor than copper, silver is very expensive, which is why copper wire is used in most electric circuits.

PAGE 38

When Ada put their circuit in the flashlight, the wires became disconnected. This broke the circuit, so the electricity stopped flowing and the light went out.

PAGE 39

They could use one of the paperclips in the drawer to make a switch for their circuit. The paperclip would need to be made of metal (a conductor) and not painted or coated with plastic (an insulator). The paperclip could be held in place with the thumbtacks and attached to the ends of both wires to complete the circuit, then moved aside to break the circuit.

PAGE 40

Buzz could make the alarm louder by adding another battery to the circuit. The more batteries you add, the greater the power.

PAGE 41

Ada and Isaac could make a battery using:

* a lemon from the fruit bowl
* the zinc nail from Ada's bag
* the copper coin from Ada's bag
* the wire from Ada's bag

They should push the nail and the coin into the lemon. Next, attach one end of each wire to the nail and the coin, and the other end to Buzz. With the two different metals (zinc and copper) as electrodes and the acid juice of the lemon as the electrolyte, this will cause electricity to flow around the circuit, giving power to Buzz.

PAGE 44

We know that magnetism can pass more easily through wood than metal, so it would be safer to hide in the wooden shack than the metal car.

PAGE 45

Hitting a magnet with a hammer or something similar will weaken or destroy its magnetism by breaking up the alignment of its particles. Ada or Isaac could grab the wooden mallet on the floor of the shack, run outside and strike the magnet until it loses enough power for Buzz to be able to escape.

PAGE 46

With magnets, unlike poles attract, and like poles repel. So North attracts South, but North repels North, and South repels South.

PAGE 47

They can use ...
* the magnet held by Ada
* the leaf floating in the puddle
* the needle Buzz is using to repair Isaac's pocket.

First, they can magnetize the needle by rubbing it against the magnet. Next, they can pick up the leaf and push the needle into it. Then they should place the leaf back on the puddle so it is floating freely there. The needle will turn around until it settles, pointing north.

PAGE 50

Another way they can strengthen the power of the electromagnet is by increasing the number of coils of wire around the bar.

PAGE 51

The crucial part that has fallen out of the drone is the electric motor. This is needed to turn the drone's propellors.

PAGE 52

The part that is missing from the alarm is the clapper that strikes the bell. It has fallen under the chair.

PAGE 53

The answer to the anagram is DYNAMO. They need this to make the hand crank mobile charger work. When Isaac turns the hand crank, it causes the dynamo's magnet to rotate, generating electricity in the coil to power the phone.

PAGE 56

The water is in the pumped storage reservoir. The words you needed to find are highlighted below:

I	E	K	A	G	L	R	O	L	O	L	G
P	V	E	E	G	S	I	K	C	E	X	O
B	U	C	M	N	S	O	L	G	V	K	O
H	L	M	G	C	C	V	A	U	J	O	M
S	T	P	P	T	U	R	B	I	N	E	J
J	G	O	T	E	O	E	T	H	R	D	U
X	U	W	D	T	D	S	Z	X	I	C	S
C	U	E	S	Z	I	E	P	N	N	D	O
U	E	R	U	Z	P	R	V	D	A	T	B
K	N	X	V	S	A	I	A	A	V	S	O
Z	K	V	T	W	M	M	R	F	U	J	R
T	Y	U	S	O	I	P	X	T	H	C	J

PAGE 57

When a turbine turns, it rotates a shaft around which copper wire is coiled. The coil of copper wire rotates within the magnetic field of powerful magnets, causing electricity to flow through the wire.

PAGE 58

Line A

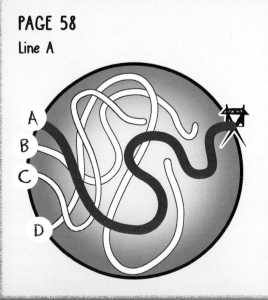

121

PAGE 59

The electricity that flows through power lines is high voltage, so transformers are needed to lower the electricity coming off the power lines to make it usable by homes and businesses. Alec Trick has switched off the transformers, so the electricity flowing into Zap City is high voltage, causing sparks to fly and fuses to blow. Ada, Isaac, and Buzz must go the electricity substations in Zap City and switch on the transformers.

CHAPTER 3

PAGE 64

The word the children were looking for was THRUST. This and the other words you needed to find are highlighted below.

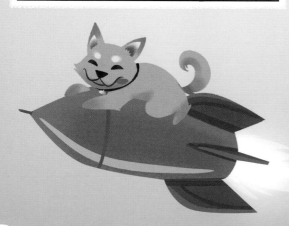

PAGE 65

Astrid has built a solid-fuel rocket engine, the kind found in early rockets. In this type of engine, the fuel and oxidizer are already mixed together as a solid. Once ignited, the engine cannot be shut off, and thrust cannot be controlled.

Astrid should build a liquid-fuel engine, where fuel and oxidizer are kept in separate chambers and are then pumped into a combustion chamber where they are mixed and burned. In a liquid-fuel engine, the amount of thrust can be controlled by varying the amount of fuel and oxidizer sent into the combustion chamber.

PAGE 66

Compared to the rocket on page 63, Anthony's design has a rather fat body and small fins. To make it more aerodynamic, he should make the body narrower. To increase stability he should make the fins bigger.

PAGE 67

Anthony has made the fins too big on this rocket. Fins give the rocket stability, but they also create drag. In this case, they gave it so much drag, the rocket fell back to Earth.

...astronauts... food and other
...stored in the middle part of the
...into the nose cone in order to
...the Artemis.

PAGE 69

The force of gravity, or g-force, on Earth
is measured at 1 g. Astronauts in a rocket
accelerating upward experience up to 3 g.
As g-forces increase, they will get "tunnel
vision" (lose the edges of their vision)
and feel sleepy. It is important to fight
sleep, tense up the body, and breathe
in short bursts, or they may "gray-out"
(everything goes gray), or "black-out" (lose
consciousness). This can cause permanent
damage or death.

PAGE 72

Artemis is being slowed down by
atmospheric drag. They need to fire
their rocket boosters to maintain their
orbital speed.

The solution to the anagram is:

FIRE ROCKET BOOSTERS

PAGE 73

Artemis is currently in a circular orbit.
It needs to move into an elliptical
orbit in order to achieve trans-lunar
injection. The Professor should press
button C.

In order to stay to stop their muscles
wasting away in microgravity, astronauts must
do regular exercise. The exercise bike Astrid
has found should help!

PAGE 75

He is connected to B.

Once he's free, Anthony can use the
jet thruster on his space suit to get
back to Artemis.

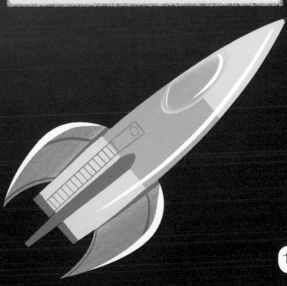

123

PAGE 76

Anthony will use the ship's radar to work out their altitude and rate of descent. Radar stands for RAdio Detection And Ranging. The ship transmits regular pulses of radio waves, which bounce off the surface of the Moon and return, like echoes, to the ship where they are picked up by a receiver. A computer then converts this data into information about *Artemis*'s height above the lunar surface and its speed of approach.

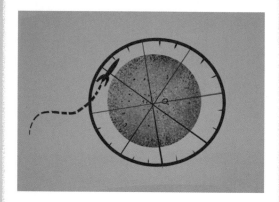

PAGE 77

The long, twisting bulge on the Moon's surface is called a lava tube. These are tubes formed by lava flows millions of years ago, when the Moon had active volcanoes. These underground tunnels provide shelter from solar radiation, meteorites, and the harsh temperatures of the lunar surface, so could be good places for a human—or an alien—to live.

PAGE 78

There are mountains on the Moon's north pole that receive almost constant sunlight, due to the motion of its orbit. The only time the sun doesn't shine in these places is during a lunar eclipse (when Earth passes between the Moon and the Sun).

PAGE 82

Akeera's explorer vessel is most likely to be on Olympus Mons, the tallest mountain on Mars and also the tallest on any planet in the solar system. Only Rheasilvia on the asteroid Vesta is higher. Olympus Mons is around 21 km (13 miles) high and 600 km (370 miles) wide. It is an extinct volcano.

PAGE 83

To make oxygen, they will need the electrolysis kit and water. By running an electric current through the water, they will separate it into its constituent elements of hydrogen and oxygen.

To grow food, they need

* seeds

* grow bags

* fertilizer and soil (to put in the grow bags)

* glue (to stick the seeds to the grow bags)

* LED lights (to give the plants energy)

PAGE 84

Average orbital velocity for an asteroid is 25 km/second. So if the asteroid is 500 km from *Artemis*, they will have 20 seconds to change course in order to avoid it.

500/25 = 20

If you are using the imperial measurements, divide 310 by 15.5. This also equals 20.

The message from the explorer vessel says they are at a "smooth place near Jupiter." This suggests they are at Europa, Jupiter's fourth-largest moon, which has the smoothest surface of any object in the Solar System.

PAGE 85

The explorer vessel's captain says they are at a "place near ringed planet with big fountains." The ringed planet is Saturn. The place near it with big fountains must be Saturn's moon Enceladus, famed for the huge plumes of water spouting from of its south polar region. These can rise up to nearly 500 km (310 miles) above the surface.

PAGE 86

They can get back to Earth using a technique called gravity assist—using the gravity of planets to increase their speed and power as they fly past them. Gravity assist was first used in 1959 by the Russian probe Luna 3 when it photographed the far side of Earth's Moon.

PAGE 87

Artemis is approaching Earth at an extremely high speed, and as it strikes the air molecules at the top of the atmosphere, this creates friction and enormous heat. To avoid burning up, the crew should turn *Artemis* 90 degrees, so that the side of the rocket faces the atmosphere. The blunt surface will slow *Artemis* down and create a shock wave that will keep the heat at a distance.

CHAPTER 4

PAGE 92

Molly should choose to write a message on the base of the copper saucepan, because copper is a soft metal. A plastic bottle is a difficult shape to write on. Steel is too hard. A message in beach sand would wash away.

PAGE 93

Tungsten may be a hard metal, but it is also brittle, so it could easily shatter. Of the other objects available, the steel rod would be the best one to use to break down the door. It is the right shape, and steel is hard.

PAGE 94

The silver foil found by Tess is reflective. They could use this as a mirror to see who's around the corner.

PAGE 95 The hidden word is "LEAD."

PAGE 96

Cloth would be a good material to use as a mask because it is permeable. This means it allows air in, so they can breathe. However, it is not too permeable, so it keeps out the most damaging fumes. Silver foil, on the other hand, is not permeable. The tungsten bowl is no use at all, since it won't even cover their mouths properly!

PAGE 97

They should use the tungsten bowl to transport the lava. Tungsten has the highest melting point of any metal. It melts at 3,422 °C (6,192 °F). This is much higher than the temperature of lava, which is 700–1,200 °C (1,292–2,192 °F).

PAGE 98

Metal is a good conductor of heat, so Molly definitely needs to put something between the tungsten bowl and her skin before carrying it. Of the materials they have with them, styrofoam would be the best insulator.

PAGE 99

They can make fresh water from the saltwater lagoon by DISTILLATION. This and the other words you needed to find are highlighted below:

X	U	O	E	O	G	X	G	D	N	R	A
A	A	P	A	L	L	U	R	I	U	M	S
R	P	S	S	R	R	N	G	S	K	S	K
G	A	D	T	E	X	I	O	T	G	E	E
P	S	P	U	T	P	P	S	I	A	G	O
O	E	R	E	A	D	A	X	L	D	C	O
A	R	E	D	W	R	S	R	L	E	X	R
G	P	G	A	T	E	E	E	A	Z	E	R
E	O	G	N	L	D	D	I	T	T	O	E
G	G	L	I	A	E	D	R	I	R	E	P
E	R	S	G	S	O	O	R	O	E	R	S
S	E	O	L	A	G	O	O	N	O	E	A

PAGE 100

The answer to the anagram is EVAPORATION. They should pour some saltwater into a bowl and use heat to turn the water into steam. This will leave a residue of salt in the bowl.

PAGE 101

No, concrete cannot be turned back into cement and water. Making concrete is an irreversible change.

PAGE 102

If they heat the ice, it will melt, not burn. Only materials containing carbon burn. When it heats up, the ice will turn into water. If they continue to heat the water, it will turn into steam.

PAGE 103

The materials in the picture that will burn are the ones containing the element carbon. They are the vegetables, the wool, the wood, the leaves, and the coal.

PAGE 106

The objects they can use to help them float when the water rises are—the barrel, the two wooden poles, and the two wedges.

PAGE 107

Tess's idea is to insert the nozzle of the bicycle pump through the cork and into the bottle. By pumping air into the bottle it will increase the air pressure inside the bottle so that the cork flies out.

PAGE 108

They could add a wheel and axle machine to the pulley. If they wound the rope around the wooden pole and then attached this to the remaining bicycle wheel, they could then turn the wheel to lift the reversium.

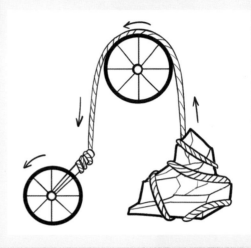

PAGE 109

They could use the two wedges. By placing one of the wedges behind each of the truck's back wheels, it would stop the truck from from falling over the cliff.

PAGE 110

Molly and Andy's parachute will work better because it has a larger surface area and a curved interior. This will help it trap more air molecules, creating greater air resistance and giving them a slower, gentler descent to the beach below.

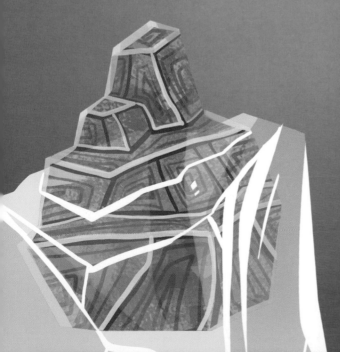

PAGE 111

They could use the wooden plank as an inclined plane. The reversium is too heavy to lift into the boat so they can slide it up the plank instead.

PAGE 115

What goes down, must come up! Molly presses a button that fills the submarine's ballast tank with air. Air is less dense than the water it displaces, and so will make the submarine rise to the surface. Once they reach the surface, the police will spot Dr. Smasher, and arrest him!

PAGE 112

A good shape for the poles would be broad and flat at the bottom where they move through the water. If they are broad and flat, this will create more water resistance, pushing the boat forward. They can use the wooden plank to improve the shape of the poles. The plank could be cut in two, and each half could be tied to one end of each of the poles with rope.

PAGE 113

They can use the steel rod as a lever to force open the hatch.

PAGE 114

They should fill the submarine's ballast tank with water. This will make the submarine denser overall than the water it has displaced, so it will sink.